WAR 1914

uncovered editions

Titles in the series

uncovered editions

WAR 1914: PUNISHING THE SERBS

London: The Stationery Office

First published 1915 Cd. 7860
© Crown Copyright

This abridged edition
© The Stationery Office 1999
Reprinted with permission.

ISBN 0 11 702410 4

A CIP catalogue record for this book is available from the
British Library.

Printed in the UK by Biddles Limited, Guildford, Surrey
J93487   C50   11/99

On June 28 1914, Archduke Franz Ferdinand, son and heir of Emperor Franz Josef, of Austria–Hungary, was assassinated in Sarajevo with his wife, Sophie, by Gavrilo Princip, a Serbian Nationalist. These papers are the diplomatic exchanges that followed. Within four weeks war broke out.

∘⟨⟩∘

Projection adjusted to show relationship of countries in this part of
south-eastern Europe (1914)

National frontiers after the Balkan wars 1912–13

Borders

LIST OF PRINCIPAL PERSONS MENTIONED IN THE CORRESPONDENCE, SHOWING THEIR OFFICIAL POSITIONS.

1. GREAT BRITAIN.

Lord High Chancellor
    Viscount Haldane.
Secretary of State for Foreign Affairs
    Sir Edward Grey.
Permanent Under-Secretary of State for Foreign Affairs.
    Sir A. Nicolson.
French Ambassador
    M. Paul Cambon.
    M. de Fleuriau (Chargé d'Affaires).
Russian Ambassador
    Count Benckendorff.
    M. de Etter (Counsellor of Embassy).

German Ambassador
> Prince Lichnowsky.

Austro-Hungarian Ambassador
> Count Mensdorff.

Belgian Minister
> Count de Lalaing.

Serbian Minister
> M. Boschkovitch.

2.   FRANCE.

President of the Republic
> M. Poincaré.

President of the Council
> M. René Viviani.

Ministers for Foreign Affairs
> 1. M. Jonnart.
> 2. M. Stéphen Pichon.
> 3. M. René Viviani.
> 4. M. Bienvenu–Martin (Acting).
> 5. M. Doumergue.
> 6. M. Delcassé.

Political Director
> M. Berthelot.

British Ambassador
> Sir Francis Bertie.

Russian Ambassador
> M. Isvolsky.
> M. Sevastopoulo (Chargé d'Affaires).

German Ambassador
> Baron von Schoen.

Austro-Hungarian Ambassador
> Count Szécsen.

Belgian Minister
> Baron Guillaume.

Serbian Minister
> M. Vesnitch.

3. RUSSIA.

Minister for Foreign Affairs
> M. Sazonof.

Minister for war
> M. Suchomlinof.

British Ambassador
> Sir George Buchanan.

French Ambassador
> M. Paléologue.

German Ambassador
> Count Pourtalès.

Austro-Hungarian Ambassador
> Count Szápáry.
> Count Czernin (Chargé d'Affaires).

Serbian Minister
> Dr. M. Spalaikovitch.

4. GERMANY.

Imperial Chancellor
> Dr. von Bethmann-Hollweg.

Secretary of State
> Herr von Jagow.

Under-Secretary of State
> Herr von Zimmermann.

British Ambassador
> Sir Edward Goschen.
> Sir Horace Rumbold (Counsellor of Embassy).

French Ambassador
   M. Jules Cambon.
   M. de Manneville (Chargé d'Affaires).
Russian Ambassador
   M. Swerbeiev.
   M. Broniewsky (Chargé d'Affaires).
American Ambassador
   Mr. Gerard.
Austro-Hungarian Ambassador
   Count Szogyeny.
Belgian Minister
   Baron Beyens.
Serbian Chargé d'Affaires
   Dr. M. Yovanovitch.
French Minister at Munich
   M. Allizé.
French Consul-General at Frankfort
   M. Ronssin.

5.   AUSTRIA-HUNGARY.
Secretary of State for Foreign Affairs
   Count Berchtold.
Under-Secretaries of State for Foreign Affairs
   Baron Macchio.
   Count Forgach.
President of the Ministry of Hungary
   Count Tisza.
British Ambassador
   Sir Maurice de Bunsen.
French Ambassador
   M. Dumaine.
Russian Ambassador

M. Schebeko.

Prince Koudacheff (Chargé d'Affaires).

American Ambassador

Mr. Penfield.

German Ambassador

Herr von Tschirscky.

Italian Ambassador

Duke d'Avarna.

Belgian Minister

Count Errembault de Dudzeele.

Serbian Minister

M.Yov. M.Yovanovitch.

French Consul-General at Buda-Pest

M. d'Apchier-le-Maugin.

Russian Consul-General at Fiume

M. Salviati.

Acting Russian Consul at Prague

M. Kazansky.

6.   TURKEY.

British Chargé d'Affaires

Mr. Beaumont.

French Ambassador

M. Bompard.

Serbian Chargé d'Affaires

M.M. Georgevitch.

Austrian Consul-General

Herr Jehlitschka.

7.   BELGIUM.

Minister for Foreign Affairs

M. Davignon.

Baron van der Elst (Secretary-General).
Colonial Minister
H. Renkin.
British Minister
Sir Francis Villiers.
French Minister
M. Klobukowski.
American Minister
Mr. Brand Whitlock.
German Minister
Herr von Below Saleske.
Austro-Hungarian Minister
Count Clary.
Dutch Minister
M. de Weede.

8. SERBIA.
Prime Minister
M. Pashitch.
Acting Prime Minister and Minister for Foreign
Affairs. Dr. Laza Patchou.
British Minister
Mr. des Graz.
Mr. Crackanthorpe (First Secretary).
French Minister
M. Boppe.
Russian Chargé d'Affaires
M. Strandtman.
German Secretary of Legation
Herr von Storck.
Austro-Hungarian Minister
Baron Giesl von Gieslingen.

Belgian Minister
    M. de Welle.

Austro-Hungarian Consular Agent at Nish
    Herr Hoflehner.

9.   ITALY.

    Minister for Foreign Affairs
        Marquis di San Giuliano.

    British Ambassador
        Sir Rennell Rodd.

    French Ambassador
        M. Barrère.

    German Ambassador
        Herr von Flotow.

    Serbian Minister
        M. Ljub Michailovitch.

10.   SPAIN.

    Belgian Minister
        Baron Grenier.

11.   DENMARK.

    French Minister
        M. Bapst.

12.   HOLLAND.

    Minister for Foreign Affairs
        M. Loudon.

    French Minister
        M. Pellet.

    Belgian Minister
        Baron Fallon.

13. LUXEMBURG.
     Minister of State and President of the
     Government Dr. Eyschen.
     French Minister
     M. Mollard.
     German Minister
     Herr von Buch.
     French Minister
     M. Chevalley.

15. SWEDEN.
     French Minister
     M. Thiébaut.

16. SWITZERLAND.
     French Consul-General at Basle
     M. Farges.

Herr Hoflehner, Consular Agent, to Count Berchtold.

Nish, July 6, 1914.

THE news of the terrible crime at Serajevo, which had
been only too successful, created here a sensation in
the fullest sense of the word. There was practically no
sign of consternation or indignation; the predominant
mood was one of satisfaction and even joy, and this
was often quite open without any reserve, and even
found expression in a brutal way. This is especially the
case with the so-called leading circles—the intellec-
tuals, such as professional politicians, those occupied

in education, officials, officers and the students. Commercial circles adopted a rather more reserved attitude.

All explanations made by official Serbian circles or individual higher personalities purporting to give expression to indignation at the crime and condemnation of it, must have the effect of the bitterest irony on anyone who has had an opportunity, during the last few days, of gaining an insight at first hand into the feelings of the educated Serbian people.

On the day of the crime the undersigned had gone to a coffee garden at about 9 o'clock in the evening without any suspicion of what had happened, and here received from an acquaintance his first information as to the very definite rumour which was being circulated. It was painful in the highest degree to see and hear what a feeling of real delight seized the numerous visitors who were present, with what obvious satisfaction the deed was discussed, and what cries of joy, scorn and contempt burst out—even one who has long been accustomed to the expression of political fanaticism which obtains here, must feel the greatest depression at what he observed.

M. N. Pashitch, Prime Minister and Minister for Foreign Affairs, to all the Royal Serbian Legations abroad.

Belgrade, June 18/July 1, 1914.

THE Austrian and Hungarian press are blaming Serbia more and more for the Serajevo outrage. Their aim is transparent, viz., to destroy that high moral reputation which Serbia now enjoys in Europe, and to take the fullest advantage politically against Serbia of the act of a young and ill-balanced fanatic. But, in Serbia itself, the Serajevo outrage has been most severely condemned in all circles of society, inasmuch as all, official as well as unofficial, immediately recognised that this outrage would be most prejudicial not only to our good neighbourly relations with Austria-Hungary but also to our co-nationalists in that country, as recent occurrences have proved. At a moment when Serbia is doing everything in her power to improve her relations with the neighbouring Monarchy, it is absurd to think that Serbia could have directly or indirectly inspired acts of this kind. On the contrary, it was of the greatest interest to Serbia to prevent the perpetration of this outrage. Unfortunately this did not lie within Serbia's power, as both assassins are Austrian subjects. Hitherto Serbia has been careful to suppress anarchic elements, and after recent events she will redouble her vigilance, and in the event of such elements existing within her borders will take the severest measures against them. Moreover, Serbia will do everything in her power and use all the means at her disposal in order to restrain the feelings of ill-balanced people within her frontiers. But Serbia can on no account permit the Vienna and Hungarian press to mislead European public opinion, and lay the heavy responsibility for a crime committed by an Austrian subject at the door of the whole Serbian nation and on Serbia, who can only suffer harm from such acts and can derive no benefit whatever.

Please act in the sense of the above views, and use all available channels in order to put an end as soon as possible to the anti-Serbian campaign in the European press.

∞◦∞

Sir Edward Grey to Sir H. Rumbold, British Chargé d'Affaires at Berlin.

Sir,

Foreign Office, July 20, 1914.

I ASKED the German Ambassador to-day if he had any news of what was going on in Vienna with regard to Serbia.

He said that he had not, but Austria was certainly going to take some step, and he regarded the situation as very uncomfortable.

I said that I had not heard anything recently, except that Count Berchtold, in speaking to the Italian Ambassador in Vienna, had deprecated the suggestion that the situation was grave, but had said that it should be cleared up.

The German Ambassador said that it would be a very desirable thing if Russia could act as a mediator with regard to Serbia.

I said that I assumed that the Austrian Government would not do anything until they had first disclosed to the public their case against Serbia, founded presumably upon what they had discovered at the trial.

The Ambassador said that he certainly assumed that they would act upon some case that would be known.

I said that this would make it easier for others, such as Russia, to counsel moderation in Belgrade. In fact, the more Austria could keep her demand within reasonable limits, and the stronger the justification she could produce for making any demand, the more chance there would be of smoothing things over. I hated the idea of a war between any of the Great Powers, and that any of them should be dragged into a war by Serbia would be detestable.

The Ambassador agreed wholeheartedly in this sentiment.

I am, &c.

E. GREY.

Sir H. Rumbold, British Chargé d'Affaires at Berlin, to Sir Edward Grey.—(Received July 22.)

(Telegraphic.) Berlin, July 22. 1914.

LAST night I met Secretary of State for Foreign Affairs, and the forthcoming Austrian *démarche* at Belgrade was alluded to by his Excellency in the conversation that ensued. His Excellency was evidently of opinion that this step on Austria's part would have been made ere this. He insisted that question at issue was one for settlement between Serbia and Austria alone, and that there should be no interference from outside in the discussions between those two countries. He had therefore considered it inadvisable that the Austro-Hungarian Government should be approached by the German Government on the matter. He had, however, on several occasions, in conversation with the Serbian Minister, emphasised the extreme importance that Austro-Serbian relations should be put on a proper footing.

Finally, his Excellency observed to me that for a long time past the attitude adopted towards Serbia by Austria had, in his opinion, been one of great forbearance.

Sir Edward Grey to Sir M. de Bunsen, British Ambassador at Vienna.

Sir, Foreign Office, July 23, 1914.

COUNT MENSDORFF told me to-day that he would be able to-morrow morning to let me have officially the

communication that he understood was being made
to Serbia to-day by Austria. He then explained privately what the nature of the demand would be. As he
told me that the facts would all be set out in the paper
that he would give me to-morrow, it is unnecessary to
record them now. I gathered that they would include
proof of the complicity of some Serbian officials in
the plot to murder the Archduke Franz Ferdinand,
and a long list of demands consequently made by
Austria on Serbia.

As regards all this, I said that it was not a matter
on which I would make any comment until I
received an official communication, and it seemed to
me probably a matter on which I should not be able
to make any comment at first sight.

But, when Count Mensdorff told me that he supposed there would be something in the nature of a
time-limit, which was in effect akin to an ultimatum,
I said that I regretted this very much. To begin with a
time-limit might inflame opinion in Russia, and it
would make it difficult, if not impossible, to give
more time, even if after a few days it appeared that by
giving more time there would be a prospect of securing a peaceful settlement and getting a satisfactory
reply from Serbia. I admitted that, if there was no
time-limit, the proceedings might be unduly pro-
tracted, but I urged that a time-limit could always be
introduced afterwards; that, if the demands were made
without a time-limit in the first instance, Russian
public opinion might be less excited, after a week it
might have cooled down, and if the Austrian case was

very strong it might be apparent that the Russian Government would be in a position to use their influence in favour of a satisfactory reply from Serbia. A time-limit was generally a thing to be used only in the last resort, after other means had been tried and failed.

Count Mensdorff said that if Serbia, in the interval that had elapsed since the murder of the Archduke, had voluntarily instituted an enquiry on her own territory, all this might have been avoided. In 1909, Serbia had said in a note that she intended to live on terms of good neighbourhood with Austria; but she had never kept her promise, she had stirred up agitation the object of which was to disintegrate Austria, and it was absolutely necessary for Austria to protect herself.

I said that I would not comment upon or criticise what Count Mensdorff had told me this afternoon, but I could not help dwelling upon the awful consequences involved in the situation. Great apprehension had been expressed to me, not specially by M. Cambon and Count Benekendorff, but also by others, as to what might happen, and it had been represented to me that it would be very desirable that those who had influence in St. Petersburgh should use it on behalf of patience and moderation. I had replied that the amount of influence that could be used in this sense would depend upon how reasonable were the Austrian demands and how strong the justification that Austria might have discovered for making her demands. The possible consequences of the present situation were terrible. If as many as four Great Powers of Europe—let us say, Austria, France, Russia, and Germany—were engaged in war, it seemed to me that it must involve the expenditure of so vast a sum of money, and such an interference with trade, that a war would be accompanied or followed by a complete collapse of European credit and industry. In these days, in great industrial States, this would mean a state of things worse than that of 1848, and, irrespective of who were victors in the war, many things might be completely swept away.

Count Mensdorff did not demur to this statement of the possible consequences of the present situation, but he said that all would depend upon Russia.

I made the remark that, in a time of difficulties such as this, it was just as true to say that it required two to keep the peace as it was to say, ordinarily, that it took two to make a quarrel. I hoped very much that, if there were difficulties, Austria and Russia would be able in the first instance to discuss them directly with each other.

Count Mensdorff said that he hoped this would be possible, but he was under the impression that the attitude in St. Petersburgh had not been very favourable recently.

I am, & c.

E. GREY.

THE AUSTRIAN NOTE

Count Berchtold, Austrian Minister for Foreign Affairs, to Count Mensdorff, Austrian Ambassador in London.— (Communicated by Count Mensdorff, July 24, 1914.) (Translation.)

THE Austro-Hungarian Government felt compelled to address the following note to the Serbian Government on the 23rd July, through the medium of the Austro-Hungarian Minister at Belgrade:—

"On the 31st March, 1909, the Serbian Minister in Vienna, on the instructions of the Serbian

Government, made the following declaration to the Imperial and Royal Government:—

"'Serbia recognises that the *fait accompli* regarding Bosnia has not affected her rights, and consequently she will conform to the decisions that the Powers may take in conformity with article 25 of the Treaty of Berlin. In deference to the advice of the Great Powers, Serbia undertakes to renounce from now onwards the attitude of protest and opposition which she has adopted with regard to the annexation since last autumn. She undertakes, moreover, to modify the direction of her policy with regard to Austria-Hungary and to live in future on good neighbourly terms with the latter.'

"The history of recent years, and in particular the painful events of the 28th June last, have shown the existence of a subversive movement with the object of detaching a part of the territories of Austria-Hungary from the Monarchy. The movement, which had its birth under the eye of the Serbian Government, has gone so far as to make itself manifest on both sides of the Serbian frontier in the shape of acts of terrorism and a series of outrages and murders.

"Far from carrying out the formal undertakings contained in the declaration of the 31st March, 1909, the Royal Serbian Government has done nothing to repress these movements. It has permitted the criminal machinations of various societies and associations directed against the Monarchy, and has tolerated unrestrained language on the part of the press, the glorification of the perpetrators of outrages, and the participation of officers and functionaries in subversive agitation. It has permitted an unwholesome propaganda in public instruction, in short, it has permitted all manifestations of a nature to incite the Serbian population to hatred of the Monarchy and contempt of its institutions.

"This culpable tolerance of the Royal Serbian Government had not ceased at the moment when the events of the 28th June last proved its fatal consequences to the whole world.

"It results from the depositions and confessions of the criminal perpetrators of the outrage of the 28th June that the Serajevo assassinations were planned in Belgrade; that the arms and explosives with which the murderers were provided had been given to them by Serbian officers and functionaries belonging to the Narodna Odbrana; and finally, that the passage into Bosnia of the criminals and their arms was organised and effected by the chiefs of the Serbian frontier service.

"The above-mentioned results of the magisterial investigation do not permit the Austro-Hungarian Government to pursue any longer the attitude of expectant forbearance which they have maintained for years in face of the machinations hatched in Belgrade, and thence propagated in the territories of the Monarchy. The results, on the contrary, impose on them the duty of putting an end to the intrigues which form a perpetual menace to the tranquillity of the Monarchy.

"To achieve this end the Imperial and Royal Government see themselves compelled to demand from the Royal Serbian Government a formal assurance that they condemn this dangerous propaganda against the Monarchy; in other words, the whole series of tendencies, the ultimate aim of which is to detach from the Monarchy territories belonging to it, and that they undertake to suppress by every means this criminal and terrorist propaganda.

"In order to give a formal character to this undertaking the Royal Serbian Government shall publish on the front page of their 'Official Journal' of the 26 July the following declaration:—

"'The Royal Government of Serbia condemn the propaganda directed against Austria-Hungary—*i.e.*, the general tendency of which the final aim is to detach from the Austro-Hungarian Monarchy territories belonging to it, and they sincerely deplore the fatal consequences of these criminal proceedings.

"'The Royal Government regret that Serbian officers and functionaries participated in the above-mentioned propaganda and thus compromised the good neighbourly relations to which the Royal Government were solemnly pledged by their declaration of the 31st March, 1909.

"'The Royal Government, who disapprove and repudiate all idea of interfering or attempting to interfere with the destinies of the inhabitants of any part whatsoever of Austria-Hungary, consider it their duty formally to warn officers and functionaries, and the whole population of the kingdom, that henceforward they will proceed with the utmost rigour against persons who may be guilty of such machinations, which they will use all their efforts to anticipate and suppress.'

"This declaration shall simultaneously be communicated to the Royal army as an order of the day by His Majesty the King and shall be published in the 'Official Bulletin' of the Army.

"The Royal Serbian Government further undertake:

"1. To suppress any publication which incites to hatred and contempt to the Austro-Hungarian Monarchy and the general tendency of which is directed against its territorial integrity;

"2. To dissolve immediately the society styled 'Narodna Odbrana,' to confiscate all its means of propaganda, and to proceed in the same manner against other societies and their branches in Serbia which engage in propaganda against the Austro-Hungarian Monarchy. The Royal Government shall take the necessary measures to prevent the societies dissolved from continuing their activity under another name and form;

"3. To eliminate without delay from public instruction in Serbia, both as regards the teaching body and also as regards the methods of instruction, everything that serves, or might serve, to foment the propaganda against Austria-Hungary;

"4. To remove from the military service, and from the administration in general, all officers and functionaries guilty of propaganda against the

Austro-Hungarian Monarchy whose names and deeds the Austro-Hungarian Government reserve to themselves the right of communicating to the Royal Government;

"5. To accept the collaboration in Serbia of representatives of the Austro-Hungarian Government for the suppression of the subversive movement directed against the territorial integrity of the Monarchy;

"6. To take judicial proceedings against accessories to the plot of the 28th June who are on Serbian territory; delegates of the Austro-Hungarian Government will take part in the investigation relating thereto;

"7. To proceed without delay to the arrest of Major Voija Tankositch and of the individual named Milan Ciganovitch, a Serbian State employé, who have been compromised by the results of the magisterial enquiry at Serajevo;

"8. To prevent by effective measures the co-operation of the Serbian authorities in the illicit traffic in arms and explosives across the frontier, to dismiss and punish severely the officials of the frontier service at Schabatz and Loznica guilty of having assisted the perpetrators of the Serajevo crime by facilitating their passage across the frontier;

"9. To furnish the Imperial and Royal Government with explanations regarding the unjustifiable utterances of high Serbian officials, both in Serbia and abroad, who, notwithstanding their official position, have not hesitated since the crime of the 28th June to express themselves in interviews in terms of hostility to the Austro-Hungarian Government; and, finally,

"10. To notify the Imperial and Royal Government without delay of the execution of the measures comprised under the preceding heads.

"The Austro-Hungarian Government expect the reply of the Royal Government at the latest by 6 o'clock on Saturday evening, the 25th July.

"A memorandum dealing with the results of the magisterial enquiry at Serajevo with regard to the officials mentioned under heads (7) and (8) is attached to this note."

I have the honour to request your Excellency to bring the contents of this note to the knowledge of the Government to which you are accredited, accompanying your communication with the following observations:—

On the 31st March, 1909, the Royal Serbian Government addressed to Austria-Hungary the declaration of which the text is reproduced above.

On the very day after this declaration Serbia embarked on a policy of instilling revolutionary ideas into the Serb subjects of the Austro-Hungarian Monarchy, and so preparing for the separation of the Austro-Hungarian territory on the Serbian frontier.

Serbia became the centre of a criminal agitation.

No time was lost in the formation of societies and groups, whose objects, either avowed or secret, was the creation of disorders on Austro-Hungarian territory. These societies and groups count among their members generals and diplomatists,

Government officials and judges—in short, men at the top of official and unofficial society in the kingdom.

Serbian journalism is almost entirely at the service of this propaganda, which is directed against Austria-Hungary, and not a day passes without the organs of the Serbian press stirring up their readers to hatred or contempt for the neighbouring Monarchy, or to outrages directed more or less openly against its security and integrity.

A large number of agents are employed in carrying on by every means the agitation against Austria-Hungary and corrupting the youth in the frontier provinces.

Since the recent Balkan crisis there has been a recrudescence of the spirit of conspiracy inherent in Serbian politicians, which has left such sanguinary imprints on the history of the kingdom; individuals belonging formerly to bands employed in Macedonia have come to place themselves at the disposal of the terrorist propaganda against Austria-Hungary.

In the presence of these doings, to which Austria-Hungary has been exposed for years, the Serbian Government have not thought it incumbent on them to take the slightest step. The Serbian Government have thus failed in the duty imposed on them by the solemn declaration of the 31st March, 1909, and acted in opposition to the will of Europe and the undertaking given to Austria-Hungary.

The patience of the Imperial and Royal Government in the face of the provocative attitude of

Serbia was inspired by the territorial disinterestedness of the Austro-Hungarian Monarchy and the hope that the Serbian Government would end in spite of everything by appreciating Austria-Hungary's friendship at its true value. By observing a benevolent attitude towards the political interests of Serbia, the Imperial and Royal Government hoped that the kingdom would finally decide to follow an analogous line of conduct on its own side. In particular, Austria-Hungary expected a development of this kind in the political ideas of Serbia, when, after the events of 1912, the Imperial and Royal Government, by its disinterested and ungrudging attitude, made such a considerable aggrandisement of Serbia possible.

The benevolence which Austria-Hungary showed towards the neighbouring State had no restraining effect on the proceedings of the kingdom, which continued to tolerate on its territory a propaganda of which the fatal consequences were demonstrated to the whole world on the 28th June last, when the Heir Presumptive to the Monarchy and his illustrious consort fell victims to a plot hatched at Belgrade.

In the presence of this state of things the Imperial and Royal Government have felt compelled to take new and urgent steps at Belgrade with a view to inducing the Serbian Government to stop the incendiary movement that is threatening the security and integrity of the Austro-Hungarian Monarchy.

The Imperial and Royal Government are convinced that in taking this step they will find themselves in full agreement with the sentiments of all civilised nations, who cannot permit regicide to become a weapon that can be employed with impunity in political strife, and the peace of Europe to be continually disturbed by movements emanating from Belgrade.

In support of the above the Imperial and Royal Government hold at the disposal of the British Government a *dossier* elucidating the Serbian intrigues and the connection between these intrigues and the murder of the 28th June.

An identical communication has been addressed to the Imperial and Royal representatives accredited to the other signatory Powers.

You are authorised to leave a copy of this despatch in the hands of the Minister for Foreign Affairs.

Vienna, July 24, 1914.

Annex

The criminal enquiry opened by the Court of Serajevo against Gavrilo Princip and his accessories in and before the act of assassination committed by them on the 28th June last has up to the present led to the following conclusions:—

1. The plot, having as its object the assassination of the Archduke Francis Ferdinand at the time of his visit to Serajevo, was formed at Belgrade by Gavrilo Princip, Nedeljko Cabrinovic, one Milau Ciganovic, and Trifko Grabez, with the assistance of Commander Voija Tankosic.

2. The six bombs and the four Browning pistols and ammunition with which the guilty parties committed the act were delivered to Princip, Cabrinovic, and Grabez by the man Milan Ciganovic and Commander Voija Tankosic at Belgrade.

3. The bombs are hand-grenades coming from the arms depôt of the Serbiau army at Kragujevac.

4. In order to ensure the success of the act, Ciganovic taught Princip, Cabrinovic, and Grabez how to use the bombs, and gave lessons in firing Browning pistols to Princip and Grabez in a forest near the shooting ground at Top-schider.

5. To enable Princip, Cabrinovic, and Grabez to cross the frontier of Bosnia-Herzegovina and smuggle in their contraband of arms secretly, a secret system of transport was organised by Ciganovic.

By this arrangement the introduction into Bosnia-Herzegovina of criminals and their arms was effected by the officials controlling the frontiers at Chabac (Rade Popovic) and Loznica, as well as by the customs officer Rudivoj Grbic, of Loznica, with the assistance of various individuals.

FRIDAY JULY 24TH

Sir Edward Grey to Sir M. de Bunsen, British Ambassador at Vienna.

(Telegraphic.)   Foreign Office, July 24, 1914.

NOTE addressed to Serbia, together with an explanation of the reasons leading up to it, has been
communicated to me by Count Mensdorff.

In the ensuing conversation with his Excellency,
I remarked that it seemed to me a matter for great
regret that a time limit, and such a short one at that,
had been insisted upon at this stage of the proceedings. The murder of the Arehduke and some of the

circumstances respecting Serbia quoted in the note aroused sympathy with Austria, as was but natural, but at the same time I had never before seen one State address to another independent State a document of so formidable a character. Demand No. 5 would be hardly consistent with the maintenance of Serbia's independent sovereignty if it were to mean, as it seemed that it might, that Austria–Hungary was to be invested with a right to appoint officials who would have authority within the frontiers of Serbia.

I added that I felt great apprehension, and that I should concern myself with the matter simply and solely from the point of view of the peace of Europe. The merits of the dispute between Austria and Serbia were not the concern of His Majesty's Government, and such comments as I had made above were not made in order to discuss those merits.

I ended by saying that doubtless we should enter into an exchange of views with other Powers, and that I must await their views as to what could be done to mitigate the difficulties of the situation.

Count Mensdorff replied that the present situation might never have arisen if Serbia had held out a hand after the murder of the Archduke; Serbia had, however, shown no sign of sympathy or help, though some weeks had already elapsed since the murder; a time limit, said his Excellency, was essential, owing to the procrastination on Serbia's part.

I said that if Serbia had procrastinated in replying, a time limit could have been introduced later; but, as things now stood, the terms of the Serbian reply had been dictated by Austria, who had not been content to limit herself to a demand for a reply within a limit of forty-eight hours from its presentation.

Sir G. Buchanan, British Ambassador at St. Petersburgh, to Sir Edward Grey.—(Received July 24.)
(Telegraphic.)   St. Petersburgh, July 24, 1914.

I HAD a telephone message this morning from M. Sazonof to the effect that the text of the Austrian ultimatum had just reached him.

His Excellency added that a reply within forty-eight hours was demanded, and he begged me to meet him at the French Embassy to discuss matters, as Austrian step clearly meant that war was imminent.

Minister for Foreign Affairs said that Austria's conduct was both provocative and immoral; she would never have taken such action unless Germany had first been consulted; some of her demands were quite impossible of acceptance. He hoped that His Majesty's Government would not fail to proclaim their solidarity with Russia and France.

The French Ambassador gave me to understand that France would fulfil all the obligations entailed by her alliance with Russia, if necessity arose, besides supporting Russia strongly in any diplomatic negotiations.

I said that I would telegraph a full report to you of what their Excellencies had just said to me. I could not, of course, speak in the name of His Majesty's Government, but personally I saw no reason to expect any declaration of solidarity from His Majesty's Government that would entail an unconditional engagement on their part to support Russia and France by force of arms. Direct British interests in Serbia were nil, and a war on behalf of that country would never be sanctioned by British public opinion. To this M. Sazonof replied that we must not forget that the general European question was involved, the Serbian question being but a part of the former, and that Great Britain could not afford to efface herself from the problems now at issue.

In reply to these remarks, I observed that I gathered from what he said that his Excellency was suggesting that Great Britain should join in making a communication to Austria to the effect that active intervention by her in the internal affairs of Serbia could not be tolerated. But supposing Austria nevertheless proceeded to embark on military measures against Serbia in spite of our representations, was it the intention of the Russian Government forthwith to declare war on Austria?

M. Sazonof said that he himself thought that Russian mobilisation would at any rate have to be carried out; but a council of Ministers was being held this afternoon to consider the whole question. A further council would be held, probably to-morrow, at which the Emperor would preside, when a decision would be come to.

I said that it seemed to me that the important point was to induce Austria to extend the time limit, and that the first thing to do was to bring an influence to bear on Austria with that end in view; French Ambassador, however, thought that either Austria had made up her mind to act at once or that she was bluffing. Whichever it might be, our only chance of averting war was for us to adopt a firm and united attitude. He did not think there was time to carry out my suggestion. Thereupon I said that it seemed to me desirable that we should know just how far Serbia was prepared to go to meet the demands formulated by Austria in her note. M. Sazonof replied that he must first consult his colleagues on this point, but that doubtless some of the Austrian demands could be accepted by Serbia.

French Ambassador and M. Sazonof both continued to press me for a declaration of complete solidarity of His Majesty's Government with French and Russian Governments, and I therefore said that it seemed to me possible that you might perhaps be willing to make strong representations to both German and Austrian Governments, urging upon them that an attack by Austria upon Serbia would endanger the whole peace of Europe. Perhaps you might see your way to saying to them that such action on the part of Austria would probably mean Russian intervention, which would involve France and Germany, and that it would be difficult for Great Britain to keep out if the war were to become general. M. Sazonof answered that we would sooner or later be dragged into war if it did break out; we should have rendered war more likely if we did not from the outset make common cause with his coun-

try and with France; at any rate, he hoped His
Majesty's Government would express strong reproba-
tion of action taken by Austria.

President of French Republic and President of
the Council cannot reach France, on their return
from Russia, for four or five days, and it looks as
though Austria purposely chose this moment to present their ultimatum.

It seems to me, from the language held by French
Ambassador, that, even if we decline to join them,
France and Russia are determined to make a strong
stand.

*Sir M. de Bunsen, British Ambassador at Vienna, to Sir
Edward Grey.—(Received July 24.)*
(Telegraphic.)   Vienna, July 24, 1914.

BEFORE departing on leave of absence, I was assured
by Russian Ambassador that any action taken by
Austria to humiliate Serbia could not leave Russia
indifferent.

Russian Chargé d'Affaires was received this
morning by Minister for Foreign Affairs, and said to
him, as his own personal view, that Austrian note was
drawn up in a form rendering it impossible of acceptance as it stood, and that it was both unusual and
peremptory in its terms. Minister for Foreign Affairs
replied that Austrian Minister was under instructions
to leave Belgrade unless Austrian demands were
accepted integrally by 4 P.M. to-morrow. His
Excellency added that Dual Monarchy felt that its

very existence was at stake; and that the step taken had caused great satisfaction throughout the country. He did not think that objections to what had been done could be raised by any Power.

Mr. Crackanthorpe, British Chargé d'Affaires at Belgrade, to Sir Edward Grey.—(Received July 24.)
(Telegraphic.)   Belgrade, July 24, 1914.

AUSTRIAN demands are considered absolutely unacceptable by Serbian Government, who earnestly trust that His Majesty's Government may see their way to induce Austrian Government to moderate them.

This request was conveyed to me by Serbian Prime Minister, who returned early this morning to Belgrade. His Excellency is dejected, and is clearly very anxious as to developments that may arise.

Note communicated by German Ambassador, July 24, 1914.

The publications of the Austro-Hungarian Government concerning the circumstances under which the assassination of the Austrian heir presumptive and his consort has taken place disclose unmistakably the aims which the Great Serbian propaganda has set itself, and the means it employs to realise them. The facts now made known must also do away with the last doubts that the centre of activity of all those tendencies which are directed towards the detachment of the Southern Slav provinces from the

Austro-Hungarian Monarchy and their incorporation into the Serbian Kingdom is to be found in Belgrade, and is at work there with at least the connivance of members of Government and army.

The Serbian intrigues have been going on for many years. In an especially marked form the Great Serbian chauvinism manifested itself during the Bosnian crisis. It was only owing to the far-reaching self-restraint and moderation of the Austro-Hungarian Government and to the energetic interference of the Great Powers that the Serbian provocations to which Austria-Hungary was then exposed did not lead to a conflict. The assurance of good conduct in future which was given by the Serbian Government at that time has not been kept. Under the eyes, at least with the tacit permission of official Serbia, the Great Serbian propaganda has continuously increased in extension and intensity; to its account must be set the recent crime, the threads of which lead to Belgrade. It has become clearly evident that it would not be consistent either with the dignity or with the self-preservation of the Austro-Hungarian Monarchy still longer to remain inactive in face of this movement on the other side of the frontier, by which the security and the integrity of her territories are constantly menaced. Under these circumstances, the course of procedure and demands of the Austro-Hungarian Government can only be regarded as equitable and moderate. In spite of that, the attitude which public opinion as well as the Government in Serbia have recently adopted does not exclude the apprehension that the Serbian Government might refuse to comply with those demands, and might allow themselves to be carried away into a provocative attitude against Austria-Hungary. The Austro-Hungarian Government, if it does not wish definitely to abandon Austria's position as a Great Power, would then have no choice but to obtain the fulfilment of their demands from the Serbian Government by strong pressure and, if necessary, by using military measures, the choice of the means having to be left to them.

The Imperial Government want to emphasise their opinion that in the present case there is only question of a matter to be settled exclusively between Austria-Hungary and Serbia, and that the Great Powers ought seriously to endeavour to reserve it to those two immediately concerned. The Imperial Government desire urgently the localisation of the conflict, because every interference of another Power would, owing to the different treaty obligations, be followed by incalculable consequences.

Sir Edward Grey to Sir F. Bertie, British Ambassador at Paris.

Sir,   Foreign Office, July 24, 1914.

AFTER telling M. Cambon to-day of the Austrian communication to Serbia, which I had received this morning, and of the comment I had made to Count Mensdorff upon it yesterday, I told M. Cambon that this afternoon I was to see the German Ambassador, who some days ago had asked me privately to exercise moderating influence in St. Petersburgh. I would say to the Ambassador that, of course, if the presentation of this ultimatum to Serbia did not lead to trouble between Austria and Russia, we need not concern ourselves about it; but, if Russia took the view of the Austrian ultimatum, which it seemed to me that any Power interested in Serbia would take, I should be quite powerless, in face of the terms of the ultimatum, to exercise any moderating influence. I would say that I thought the only chance of any mediating or moderating influence being exercised was that Germany, France, Italy, and ourselves, who had not direct interests in Serbia, should act together for the sake of peace, simultaneously in Vienna and St. Petersburgh.

M. Cambon said that, if there was a chance of mediation by the four Powers, he had no doubt that his Government would be glad to join in it; but he pointed out that we could not say anything in St. Petersburgh till Russia had expressed some opinion or taken some action. But, when two days were over, Austria would march into Serbia, for the Serbians could not possibly accept the Austrian demand. Russia would be compelled by her public opinion to take action as soon as Austria attacked Serbia, and therefore, once the Austrians had attacked Serbia, it would be too late for any mediation.

I said that I had not contemplated anything being said in St. Petersburgh until after it was clear that there must be trouble between Austria and Russia. I had thought that if Austria did move into Serbia, and Russia then mobilised, it would be possible for the four Powers to urge Austria to stop her advance, and Russia also to stop hers, pending mediation. But it would be essential for any chance of success for such a step that Germany should participate in it.

M. Cambon said that it would be too late after Austria had once moved against Serbia. The important thing was to gain time by mediation in Vienna. The best chance of this being accepted would be that Germany should propose it to the other Powers.

I said that by this he meant a mediation between Austria and Serbia.

He replied that it was so.

I said that I would talk to the German Ambassador this afternoon on the subject.

I am, &c.

E. GREY.

Sir Edward Grey to Sir H. Rumbold, British Chargé d'Affaires at Berlin.
(Telegraphic.)   Foreign Office, July 24, 1914.

GERMAN Ambassador has communicated to me the view of the German Government about the Austrian demand in Serbia. I understand the German Government is making the same communication to the Powers.

I said that if the Austrian ultimatum to Serbia did

not lead to trouble between Austria and Russia I had no concern with it; I had heard nothing yet from St. Petersburgh, but I was very apprehensive of the view Russia would take of the situation. I reminded the German Ambassador that some days ago he had expressed a personal hope that if need arose I would endeavour to exercise moderating influence at St. Petersburgh, but now I said that, in view of the extra-ordinarily stiff character of the Austrian note, the shortness of the time allowed, and the wide scope of the demands upon Serbia, I felt quite helpless as far as Russia was concerned, and I did not believe any Power could exercise influence alone.

The only chance I could see of mediating or moderating influence being effective, was that the four Powers, Germany, Italy, France, and ourselves, should work together simultaneously at Vienna and St. Petersburgh in favour of moderation in the event of the relations between Austria and Russia becoming threatening.

The immediate danger was that in a few hours Austria might march into Serbia and Russian Slav opinion demand that Russia should march to help Serbia; it would be very desirable to get Austria not to precipitate military action and so to gain more time. But none of us could influence Austria in this direction unless Germany would propose and participate in such action at Vienna. You should inform Secretary of State.

Prince Lichnowsky said that Austria might be expected to move when the time limit expired unless

Serbia could give unconditional acceptance of Austrian demands *in toto*. Speaking privately, his Excellency suggested that a negative reply must in no case be returned by Serbia; a reply favourable on some points must be sent at once, so that an excuse against immediate action might be afforded to Austria.

Sir Edward Grey to Mr. Crackanthorpe, British Chargé d'Affaires at Belgrade.
(Telegraphic.)   Foreign Office, July 24, 1914.

Serbia ought to promise that, if it is proved that Serbian officials, however subordinate they may be, were accomplices in the murder of the Archduke at Serajevo, she will give Austria the fullest satisfaction. She certainly ought to express concern and regret. For the rest, Serbian Government must reply to Austrian demands as they consider best in Serbian interests.

It is impossible to say whether military action by Austria when time limit expires can be averted by anything but unconditional acceptance of her demands, but only chance appears to lie in avoiding an absolute refusal and replying favourably to as many points as the time limit allows.

Serbian Minister here has begged that His Majesty's Government will express their views, but I cannot undertake responsibility of saying more than I have said above, and I do not like to say even that without knowing what is being said at Belgrade by French and Russian Governments. You should therefore consult your French and Russian colleagues as to repeating what my views are, as expressed above, to Serbian Government.

I have urged upon German Ambassador that Austria should not precipitate military action.

Note communicated by Russian Ambassador, July 25.
(Translation.)

SATURDAY JULY 25TH

M. SAZONOF telegraphs to the Russian Chargé d'Affaires at Vienna on the 11th (24th) July, 1914.

'The communication made by Austria-Hungary to the Powers the day after the presentation of the ultimatum at Belgrade leaves a period to the Powers which is quite insufficient to enable them to take any steps which might help to smooth away the difficulties that have arisen.

'In order to prevent the consequences, equally incalculable and fatal to all the Powers, which may result from the course of action followed by the Austro-Hungarian Government, it seems to us to be above all essential that the period allowed for the Serbian reply should be extended. Austria-Hungary, having declared her readiness to inform the Powers of the results of the enquiry upon which the Imperial and Royal Government base their accusations, should equally allow them sufficient time to study them.

"In this case, if the Powers were convinced that certain of the Austrian demands were well founded, they would be in a position to offer advice to the Serbian Government.

"A refusal to prolong the term of the ultimatum would render nugatory the proposals made by the Austro-Hungarian Government to the Powers, and would be in contradiction to the very bases of international relations.

"Prince Kudachef is instructed to communicate the above to the Cabinet at Vienna."

M. Sazonof hopes that His Britannic Majesty's Government will adhere to the point of view set forth above, and he trusts that Sir E. Grey will see his way to furnish similar instructions to the British Ambassador at Vienna.

Sir Edward Grey to Sir F. Bertie, British Ambassador at Paris, and to Sir G. Buchanan, British Ambassador at St. Petersburgh.
(Telegraphic.)   Foreign Office, July 25, 1914.

AUSTRIAN Ambassador has been authorised to explain to me that the step taken at Belgrade was not an ultimatum, but a *démarche* with a time limit, and that if the Austrian demands were not complied with within the time limit the Austro-Hungarian Government would break off diplomatic relations and begin military preparations, not operations.

In case Austro-Hungarian Government have not given the same information at Paris (St. Petersburgh), you should inform Minister for Foreign Affairs as soon as possible; it makes the immediate situation rather less acute.

Sir F. Bertie, British Ambassador at Paris, to Sir Edward Grey.—(Received July 25.)
(Telegraphic.)   Paris, July 25, 1914.

I LEARN from the Acting Political Director that the French Government have not yet received the explanation from the Austrian Government contained in your telegram of to-day. They have, however, through the Serbian Minister here, given similar advice to Serbia as was contained in your telegram to Belgrade of yesterday.

Sir F. Bertie, British Ambassador at Paris, to Sir Edward Grey.—(Received July 25.)
(Telegraphic.)   Paris, July 25, 1914.

ACTING Minister for Foreign Affairs has no suggestions to make except that moderating advice might be given at Vienna as well as Belgrade. He hopes that the Serbian Government's answer to the Austrian ultimatum will be sufficiently favourable to obviate extreme measures being taken by the Austrian Government. He says, however, that there would be a revolution in Serbia if she were to accept the Austrian demands in their entirety.

Sir G. Buchanan, British Ambassador at St. Petersburgh, to Sir Edward Grey.—(Received July 25.)
(Telegraphic.)   St. Petersburgh, July 25, 1914.

I SAW the Minister for Foreign Affairs this morning, and communicated to his Excellency the substance of your telegram of to-day to Paris, and this afternoon I discussed with him the communication which the French Ambassador suggested should be made to the Serbian Government, as recorded in your telegram of yesterday to Belgrade.

The Minister for Foreign Affairs said, as regards the former, that the explanations of the Austrian Ambassador did not quite correspond with the information which had reached him from German quarters. As regards the latter, both his Excellency and the French Ambassador agreed that it is too late to make such a communication, as the time limit expires this evening.

The Minister for Foreign Affairs said that Serbia was quite ready to do as you had suggested and to punish those proved to be guilty, but that no independent State could be expected to accept the political demands which had been put forward. The Minister for Foreign Affairs thought, from a conversation which he had with the Serbian Minister yesterday, that, in the event of the Austrians attacking Serbia, the Serbian Government would abandon Belgrade, and withdraw their forces into the interior, while they would at the same time appeal to the Powers to help them. His Excellency was in favour of their making this appeal. He would like to see the question placed on an international footing, as the obligations taken by Serbia in 1908, to which reference is made in the Austrian ultimatum, were given not to Austria, but to the Powers.

If Serbia should appeal to the Powers, Russia would be quite ready to stand aside and leave the question in the hands of England, France, Germany, and Italy. It was possible, in his opinion, that Serbia might propose to submit the question to arbitration.

On my expressing the earnest hope that Russia would not precipitate war by mobilising until you had had time to use your influence in favour of peace, his Excellency assured me that Russia had no aggressive intentions, and she would take no action until it was forced upon her. Austria's action was in reality directed against Russia. She aimed at overthrowing the present *status quo* in the Balkans, and establishing her own hegemony there. He did not believe that Germany really wanted war, but her attitude was decided by ours. If we took our stand firmly with France and Russia there would be no war. If we failed them now, rivers of blood would flow, and we would in the end be dragged into war.

I said that England could play the rôle of mediator at Berlin and Vienna to better purpose as friend who, if her counsels of moderation were disregarded, might one day be converted into an ally, than if she were to declare herself Russia's ally at once. His Excellency said that unfortunately Germany was convinced that she could count upon our neutrality.

I said all I could to impress prudence on the Minister for Foreign Affairs, and warned him that if Russia mobilised, Germany would not be content with mere mobilisation, or give Russia time to carry out hers, but would probably declare war at once. His Excellency replied that Russia could not allow Austria to crush Serbia and become the predominant Power in the Balkans, and, if she feels secure of the support of France, she will face all the risks of war. He assured me once more that he did not wish to precipitate a conflict, but that unless Germany could restrain Austria I could regard the situation as desperate.

Sir H. Rumbold, British Chargé d'Affaires at Berlin, to Sir Edward Grey.—(Received July 25.)
(Telegraphic.)   Berlin, July 25, 1914.

YOUR telegram of the 24th July acted on.

Secretary of State says that on receipt of a telegram at 10 this morning from German Ambassador at London, he immediately instructed German Ambassador at Vienna to pass on to Austrian Minister for Foreign Affairs your suggestion for an extension of time limit, and to speak to his Excellency about it. Unfortunately it appeared from press that Count Berchtold is at Ischl, and Secretary

of State thought that in these circumstances there
would be delay and difficulty in getting time limit
extended. Secretary of State said that he did not know
what Austria-Hungary had ready on the spot, but he
admitted quite freely that Austro-Hungarian
Government wished to give the Serbians a lesson, and
that they meant to take military action. He also
admitted that Serbian Government could not swallow
certain of the Austro-Hungarian demands.

Secretary of State said that a reassuring feature of
situation was that Count Berchtold had sent for
Russian representative at Vienna and had told him
that Austria-Hungary had no intention of seizing
Serbian territory. This step should, in his opinion,
exercise a calming influence at St. Petersburgh. I asked
whether it was not to be feared that, in taking military action against Serbia, Austria would dangerously
excite public opinion in Russia. He said he thought
not. He remained of opinion that crisis could be
localised. I said that telegrams from Russia in this
morning's papers did not look very reassuring, but he
maintained his optimistic view with regard to Russia.
He said that he had given the Russian Government
to understand that last thing Germany wanted was a
general war, and he would do all in his power to prevent such a calamity. If the relations between Austria
and Russia became threatening, he was quite ready to
fall in with your suggestion as to the four Powers
working in favour of moderation at Vienna and St.
Petersburgh.

Secretary of State confessed privately that he

thought the note left much to be desired as a diplomatic document. He repeated very earnestly that, though he had been accused of knowing all about the contents of that note, he had in fact had no such knowledge.

Sir R. Rodd, British Ambassador at Rome, to Sir Edward Grey.—(Received July 25.)
(Telegraphic.)   Rome, July 25, 1914.

I SAW the Secretary-General this morning and found that he knew of the suggestion that France, Italy, Germany, and ourselves should work at Vienna and St. Petersburgh in favour of moderation, if the relations between Austria and Serbia become menacing.

In his opinion Austria will only be restrained by the unconditional acceptance by the Serbian Government of her note. There is reliable information that Austria intends to seize the Salonica Railway.

Sir M. de Bunsen, British Ambassador at Vienna, to Sir Edward Grey.—(Received July 25.)
(Telegraphic.)   Vienna, July 25, 1914.

LANGUAGE of press this morning leaves the impression that the surrender of Serbia is neither expected nor really desired. It is officially announced that the Austrian Minister is instructed to leave Belgrade with staff of legation failing unconditional acceptance of note at 6 P.M. to-day.

Minister for Foreign Affairs goes to Ischl to-day

to communicate personally to the Emperor Serbian reply when it comes.

Mr. Crackanthorpe, British Chargé d'Affaires at Belgrade, to Sir Edward Grey.—(Received July 25.)
(Telegraphic.)   Belgrade, July 25, 1914.

THE Council of Ministers is now drawing up their reply to the Austrian note. I am informed by the Under-Secretary of State for Foreign Affairs that it will be most conciliatory and will meet the Austrian demands in as large a measure as is possible.

The following is a brief summary of the projected reply:—

The Serbian Government consent to the publication of a declaration in the "Official Gazette." The ten points are accepted with reservations. Serbian Government declare themselves ready to agree to a mixed commission of enquiry so long as the appointment of the commission can be shown to be in accordance with international usage. They consent to dismiss and prosecute those officers who can be clearly proved to be guilty, and they have already arrested the officer referred to in the Austrian note. They are prepared to suppress the Narodna Odbrana.

The Serbian Government consider that, unless the Austrian Government want war at any cost, they cannot but be content with the full satisfaction offered in the Serbian reply.

Mr. Crackanthorpe, British Chargé d'Affaires at Belgrade, to Sir Edward Grey.—(Received July 25.)
(Telegraphic.)   Belgrade, July 25, 1914.

I HAVE seen the new French Minister, who has just arrived from Constantinople, and my Russian colleague, and informed them of your views.

They have not yet received instructions from their Governments, and in view of this and of the proposed conciliatory terms of the Serbian reply, I have up to now abstained from offering advice to the Serbian Government.

I think it is highly probable that the Russian Government have already urged the utmost moderation on the Serbian Government.

Mr. Crackanthorpe, British Chargé d'Affaires at Belgrade, to Sir Edward Grey.—(Received July 25.)
(Telegraphic.)   Belgrade, July 25, 1914.

THE Austrian Minister left at 6.30.

The Government have left for Nish, where the Skuptchina (the Serbian Parliament) will meet on Monday. I am leaving with my other colleagues, but the vice-consul is remaining in charge of the archives.

Sir Edward Grey to Sir G. Buchanan, British Ambassador at St. Petersburgh.
(Telegraphic.)   Foreign Office, July 25, 1914.

YOU spoke quite rightly in very difficult circumstances as to the attitude of His Majesty's

Government. I entirely approve what you said, as reported in your telegram of yesterday, and I cannot promise more on behalf of the Government.

I do not consider that public opinion here would or ought to sanction our going to war over a Serbian quarrel. If, however, war does take place, the development of other issues may draw us into it, and I am therefore anxious to prevent it.

The sudden, brusque, and peremptory character of the Austrian *démarche* makes it almost inevitable that in a very short time both Russia and Austria will have mobilised against each other. In this event, the only chance of peace, in my opinion, is for the other four Powers to join in asking the Austrian and Russian Governments not to cross the frontier, and to give time for the four Powers acting at Vienna and St. Petersburgh to try and arrange matters. If Germany will adopt this view, I feel strongly that France and ourselves should act upon it. Italy would no doubt gladly co-operate.

No diplomatic intervention or mediation would be tolerated by either Russia or Austria unless it was clearly impartial and included the allies or friends of both. The co-operation of Germany would, therefore, be essential.

Sir Edward Grey to Sir H. Rumbold, British Chargé d'Affaires at Berlin.
(Telegraphic.)   Foreign Office, July 25, 1914.

THE Austrian Ambassador has been authorised to inform me that the Austrian method of procedure on expiry of the time limit would be to break off diplomatic relations and commence military preparations, but not military operations. In informing the German Ambassador of this, I said that it interposed a stage of mobilisation before the frontier was actually crossed, which I had urged yesterday should be delayed.

Apparently we should now soon be face to face with the mobilisation of Austria and Russia. The only chance of peace, if this did happen, would be for Germany, France, Italy and ourselves to keep together, and to join in asking Austria and Russia not to cross the frontier till we had time to try and arrange matters between them.

The German Ambassador read me a telegram from the German Foreign Office saying that his Government had not known beforehand, and had had no more than other Powers to do with the stiff terms of the Austrian note to Serbia, but once she had launched that note, Austria could not draw back. Prince Lichnowsky said, however, that if what I contemplated was mediation between Austria and Russia, Austria might be able with dignity to accept it. He expressed himself as personally favourable to this suggestion.

I concurred in his observation, and said that I felt I had no title to intervene between Austria and Serbia, but as soon as the question became one as between Austria and Russia, the peace of Europe was affected, in which we must all take a hand.

I impressed upon the Ambassador that, in the event of Russian and Austrian mobilisation, the participation of Germany would be essential to any diplomatic action for peace. Alone we could do nothing. The French Government were travelling at the moment, and I had had no time to consult them, and could not therefore be sure of their views, but I was prepared, if the German Government agreed with my suggestion, to tell the French Government that I thought it the right thing to act upon it.

Sir Edward Grey to Sir M. de Bunsen, British Ambassador at Vienna.

(Telegraphic.)   Foreign Office, July 25, 1914.

THE Russian Ambassador has communicated to me the following telegram which his Government have sent to the Russian Ambassador at Vienna, with instructions to communicate it to the Austrian Minister for Foreign Affairs:—

"The delay given to Serbia for a reply is so limited that the Powers are prevented from taking any steps to avert the complications which are threatening. The Russian Government trust that the Austrian Government will prolong the time limit, and as the latter have declared their willingness to inform the Powers of the data on which they have based their demands on Serbia, the Russian Government hope that these particulars will be furnished in order that the Powers may examine the matter. If they found that some of the Austrian requests were well founded, they would be in a position to advise the Serbian Government accordingly. If the Austrian Government were indisposed to prolong the time limit, not only would they be acting against international ethics, but they would deprive their communication to the Powers of any practical meaning."

You may support in general terms the step taken by your Russian colleague.

Since the telegram to the Russian Ambassador at Vienna was sent, it has been a relief to hear that the steps which the Austrian Government were taking were to be limited for the moment to the rupture of relations and to military preparations, and not operations. I trust, therefore, that if the Austro-Hungarian Government consider it too late to prolong the time limit, they will at any rate give time in the sense and for the reasons desired by Russia before taking any irretrievable steps.

Sir Edward Grey to Sir F. Bertie, British Ambassador at Paris, Sir H. Rumbold, British Chargé d'Affaires at Berlin, and Sir G. Buchanan, British Ambassador at St. Petersburgh.

(Telegraphic.) Foreign Office, July 25, 1914.

I HAVE communicated to German Ambassador the forecast of the Serbian reply contained in Mr. Crackanthorpe's telegram of to-day. I have said that, if Serbian reply, when received at Vienna, corresponds to this forecast, I hope the German Government will feel able to influence the Austrian Government to take a favourable view of it..

Sir Edward Grey to Sir R. Rodd, British Ambassador at Rome.

Sir,   Foreign Office, July 25, 1914.

THE Italian Ambassador came to see me to-day. I told him in general terms what I had said to the German Ambassador this morning.

The Italian Ambassador cordially approved of this. He made no secret of the fact that Italy was most desirous to see war avoided.

I am, &c.

E. GREY.

Sir Edward Grey to Mr. Crackanthorpe, British Chargé d'Affaires at Belgrade.

Sir,   Foreign Office, July 25, 1914.

THE Serbian Minister called on the 23rd instant and spoke to Sir A. Nicolson on the present strained relations between Serbia and Austria-Hungary.

He said that his Government were most anxious and disquieted. They were perfectly ready to meet any reasonable demands of Austria-Hungary so long as such demands were kept on the "terrain juridique." If the results of the enquiry at Serajevo—an enquiry conducted with so much mystery and secrecy—disclosed the fact that there were any individuals conspiring or organising plots on Serbian territory, the Serbian Government would be quite ready to take the necessary steps to give satisfaction; but if Austria transported the question on to the political ground, and said that Serbian policy, being inconvenient to her, must undergo a radical change, and that Serbia must abandon certain political ideals, no independent State would, or could, submit to such dictation.

He mentioned that both the assassins of the Archduke were Austrian subjects—Bosniaks; that one of them had been in Serbia, and that the Serbian authorities, considering him suspect and dangerous, had desired to expel him, but on applying to the Austrian authorities found that the latter protected him, and said that he was an innocent and harmless individual.

Sir A. Nicolson, on being asked by M. Boschkovitch his opinion on the whole question, observed that there were no data on which to base one, though it was to be hoped that the Serbian Government would endeavour to meet the Austrian demands in a conciliatory and moderate spirit.

I am, &c.

E. GREY.

SUNDAY JULY 26TH

Sir M. de Bunsen, British Ambassador at Vienna, to Sir Edward Grey.—(Received July 26.)
(Telegraphic.)   Vienna, July 25, 1914.

Serbian reply to the Austro-Hungarian demands is not considered satisfactory, and the Austro-Hungarian Minister has left Belgrade. War is thought to be imminent.

Sir M. de Bunsen, British Ambassador at Vienna, to Sir Edward Grey.—(Received July 26.)
(Telegraphic.)   Vienna, July 26, 1914.

ACCORDING to confident belief of German Ambassador, Russia will keep quiet during chastisement of Serbia, which Austria-Hungary is resolved to inflict, having received assurances that no Serbian territory will be annexed by Austria-Hungary. In reply to my question whether Russian Government might not be compelled by public opinion to intervene on behalf of kindred nationality, he said that everything depended on the personality of the Russian Minister for Foreign Affairs, who could resist easily, if he chose, the pressure of a few newspapers. He pointed out that the days of Pan-Slav agitation in Russia were over and that Moscow was perfectly quiet. The Russian Minister for Foreign Affairs would not, his Excellency thought, be so imprudent as to take a step which would probably result in many frontier questions in which Russia is interested, such as Swedish, Polish, Ruthene, Roumanian, and Persian questions being brought into the melting-pot. France, too, was not at all in a condition for facing a war.

I replied that matters had, I thought, been made a little difficult for other Powers by the tone of Austro-Hungarian Government's ultimatum to Serbia. One naturally sympathised with many of the requirements of the ultimatum, if only the manner of expressing them had been more temperate. It was, however, impossible, according to the German Ambassador, to speak effectively in any other way to Serbia. Serbia was about to receive a lesson which she required; the quarrel, however, ought not to be extended in any way to foreign countries. He doubted Russia, who had no right to assume a protectorate over Serbia, act-ing as if she made any such claim. As for Germany she knew very well what she was about in backing up Austria-Hungary in this matter.

The German Ambassador had heard of a letter addressed by you yesterday to the German Ambassador in London in which you expressed the hope that the Serbian concessions would be regarded as satisfactory. He asked whether I had been informed that a pretence of giving way at the last moment had been made by the Serbian Government. I had, I said, heard that on practically every point Serbia had been willing to give in. His Excellency replied that Serbian concessions were all a sham. Serbia proved that she well knew that they were insufficient to satisfy the legitimate demands of Austria-Hungary by the fact that before making her offer she had ordered mobil-isation and retirement of Government from Belgrade.

Sir H. Rumbold, British Chargé d'Affaires at Berlin, to Sir Edward Grey.—(Received July 26.)
(Telegraphic.) Berlin, July 26, 1914.

EMPEROR returns suddenly to-night, and Under-Secretary of State says that Foreign Office regret this step, which was taken on His Majesty's own initiative. They fear that His Majesty's sudden return may cause speculation and excitement. Under-Secretary of State likewise told me that German Ambassador at St. Petersburgh had reported that, in conversation with Russian Minister for Foreign Affairs, latter had said that if Austria annexed bits of Serbian territory Russia would not remain indifferent. Under-Secretary of State drew conclusion that Russia would not act if Austria did not annex territory.

Sir H. Rumbold, British Chargé d'Affaires at Berlin, to Sir Edward Grey.—(Received July 26.)
(Telegraphic.)   Berlin, July 26, 1914.

UNDER-SECRETARY of State has just telephoned to me to say that German Ambassador at Vienna has been instructed to pass on to Austro-Hungarian Government your hopes that they may take a favourable view of Serbian reply if it corresponds to the forecast contained in Belgrade telegram of 25th July.

Under-Secretary of State considers very fact of their making this communication to Austro-Hungarian Government implies that they associate themselves to a certain extent with your hope. German Government do not see their way to going beyond this.

Sir R. Rodd, British Ambassador at Rome, to Sir Edward Grey.—(Received July 26.)
(Telegraphic.)   Rome, July 26, 1914.

MINISTER for Foreign Affairs welcome your proposal for a conference, and will instruct Italian Ambassador to-night accordingly.

Austrian Ambassador has informed Italian

Government this evening that Minister in Belgrade had been recalled, but that this did not imply declaration of war.

Sir Edward Grey to Sir F. Bertie, British Ambassador at Paris, Sir H. Rumbold, British Chargé d'Affaires at Berlin, and Sir R. Rodd, British Ambassador at Rome.
(Telegraphic.)   Foreign Office, July 26, 1914.

WOULD Minister for Foreign Affairs be disposed to instruct Ambassador here to join with representatives of France, Italy, and Germany, and myself to meet here in conference immediately for the purpose of discovering an issue which would prevent complications? You should ask Minister for Foreign Affairs whether he would do this. If so, when bringing the above suggestion to the notice of the Governments to which they are accredited, representatives at Belgrade, Vienna, and St. Petersburgh should be authorised to request that all active military operations should be suspended pending results of conference.

Sir Edward Grey to Sir F. Bertie, British Ambassador at Paris.
(Telegraphic.)   Foreign Office, July 26, 1914.

BERLIN telegram of 25th July.

It is important to know if France will agree to suggested action by the four Powers if necessary.

Sir R. Rodd, British Ambassador at Rome, to Sir Edward Grey.—(Received July 27.)

Sir,   Rome, July 23, 1914.

I GATHER that the Italian Government have been made cognisant of the terms of the communication which will be addressed to Serbia. Secretary-General, whom I saw this morning at the Italian Foreign Office, took the view that the gravity of the situation lay in the conviction of the Austro-Hungarian Government that it was absolutely necessary for their prestige, after the many disillusions which the turn of events in the Balkans has occasioned, to score a definite success.

I have, &c.

RENNELL RODD.

MONDAY JULY 27TH

THE SERBIAN REPLY

Reply of Serbian Government to Austro-Hungarian Note.—(Communicated by the Serbian Minister, July 27.) (Translation.)

THE Royal Serbian Government have received the communication of the Imperial and Royal Government of the 10th instant, and are convinced that their reply will remove any misunderstanding which may threaten to impair the good neighbourly relations between the Austro-Hungarian Monarchy and the Kingdom of Serbia.

Conscious of the fact that the protests which were made both from the tribune of the national Skuptchina and in the declarations and actions of the responsible representatives of the State—protests which were cut short by the declarations made by the Serbian Government on the 18th March, 1909—have not been renewed on any occasion as regards the great neighbouring Monarchy, and that no attempt has been made since that time, either by the successive Royal Governments or by their organs, to change the political and legal state of affairs created in Bosnia and Herzegovina, the Royal Government draw attention to the fact that in this connection the Imperial and Royal Government have made no representation except one concerning a school book, and that on that occasion the Imperial and Royal Government received an entirely satisfactory explanation. Serbia has several times given proofs of her pacific and moderate policy during the Balkan crisis, and it is thanks to Serbia and to the sacrifice that she has made in the exclusive interest of European peace that that peace has been preserved. The Royal Government cannot be held responsible for manifestations of a private character, such as articles in the press and the peaceable work of societies—manifestations which take place in nearly all countries in the ordinary course of events, and which, as a general rule, escape official control. The Royal Government are all the less responsible, in view of the fact that at the time of the solution of a series of questions which arose between Serbia and Austria-Hungary they gave proof of a great readiness to oblige, and thus succeeded in settling the majority of these questions to the advantage of the two neighbouring countries.

For these reasons the Royal Government have been pained and surprised at the statements, according to which members of the Kingdom of Serbia are supposed to have participated in the preparations for the crime committed at Serajevo; the Royal Government expected to be invited to collaborate in an investigation of all that concerns this crime, and they were ready, in order to prove the entire correctness of their attitude, to take measures against any persons concerning whom representations were made to them. Falling in, therefore, with the desire of the Imperial and Royal Government, they are prepared to hand over for trial any Serbian subject, without regard to his situation or rank, of whose complicity in the crime of Serajevo proofs are forth-coming, and more especially they undertake to cause to be published on the first page of the "Journal officiel," on the date of the 26th July, the following declaration:—

"The Royal Government of Serbia condemn all propaganda which may be directed against Austria-Hungary, that is to say, all such tendencies as aim at ultimately detaching from the Austro-Hungarian Monarchy territories which form part thereof, and they sincerely deplore the baneful consequences of these criminal movements. The Royal Government regret that, according to the communication from the

Imperial and Royal Government, certain Serbian officers and officials should have taken part in the
above-mentioned propaganda, and thus compromised
the good neighbourly relations to which the Royal
Serbian Government was solemnly engaged by the
declaration of the 31st March, 1909, which declaration
disapproves and repudiates all idea or attempt at interference with the destiny of the inhabitants of any part
whatsoever of Austria-Hungary, and they consider it
their duty formally to warn the officers, officials and
entire population of the kingdom that henceforth they
will take the most rigorous steps against all such persons as are guilty of such acts, to prevent and to repress
which they will use their utmost endeavour."

This declaration will be brought to the knowledge of the Royal Army in an order of the day, in the
name of His Majesty the King, by his Royal Highness
the Crown Prince Alexander, and will be published in
the next official army bulletin.

The Royal Government further undertake:—

To introduce at the first regular convocation of
the Skuptchina a provision into the press law providing for the most severe punishment of incitement to
hatred or contempt of the Austro-Hungarian
Monarchy, and for taking action against any publication the general tendency of which is directed against
the territorial integrity of Austria-Hungary. The
Government engage at the approaching revision of
the Constitution to cause an amendment to be introduced into article 22 of the Constitution of such a
nature that such publication may be confiscated, a

proceeding at present impossible under the categorical terms of article 22 of the Constitution.

The Government possess no proof, nor does the
note of the Imperial and Royal Government furnish
them with any, that the "Narodna Odbrana" and
other similar societies have committed up to the present any criminal act of this nature through the
proceedings of any of their members. Nevertheless,
the Royal Government will accept the demand of the
Imperial and Royal Government, and will dissolve
the "Narodna Odbrana" Society and every other
society which may be directing its efforts against
Austria-Hungary.

The Royal Serbian Government undertake to
remove without delay from their public educational
establishments in Serbia all that serves or could serve
to foment propaganda against Austria-Hungary,
whenever the Imperial and Royal Government furnish them with facts and proofs of this propaganda.

The Royal Government also agree to remove
from military service all such persons as the judicial
enquiry may have proved to be guilty of acts directed
against the integrity of the territory of the Austro-
Hungarian Monarchy, and they expect the Imperial
and Royal Government to communicate to them at a
later date the names and the acts of these officers and
officials for the purposes of the proceedings which
are to be taken against them.

The Royal Government must confess that they
do not clearly grasp the meaning or the scope of the
demand made by the Imperial and Royal

Government that Serbia shall undertake to accept the collaboration of the organs of the Imperial and Royal Government upon their territory, but they declare that they will admit such collaboration as agrees with the principle of international law, with criminal procedure, and with good neighbourly relations.

It goes without saying that the Royal Government consider it their duty to open an enquiry against all such persons as are, or eventually may be, implicated in the plot of the 15th June, and who happen to be within the territory of the kingdom. As regards the participation in this enquiry of Austro-Hungarian agents or authorities appointed for this purpose by the Imperial and Royal Government, the Royal Government cannot accept such an arrangement, as it would be a violation of the Constitution and of the law of criminal procedure; nevertheless, in concrete cases communications as to the results of the investigation in question might be given to the Austro-Hungarian agents.

The Royal Government proceeded, on the very evening of the delivery of the note, to arrest Commandant Voislav Tankossitch. As regards Milan Ziganovitch, who is a subject of the Austro-Hungarian Monarchy and who up to the 15th June was employed (on probation) by the directorate of railways, it has not yet been possible to arrest him.

The Austro-Hungarian Government are requested to be so good as to supply as soon as possible, in the customary form, the pre-sumptive evidence of guilt, as well as the eventual proofs of guilt which have been collected up to the present, at the enquiry at Serajevo for the purposes of the later enquiry.

The Serbian Government will reinforce and extend the measures which have been taken for preventing the illicit traffic of arms and explosives across the frontier. It goes without saying that they will immediately order an enquiry and will severely punish the frontier officials on the Schabatz-Loznitza line who have failed in their duty and allowed the authors of the crime of Serajevo to pass.

The Royal Government will gladly give explanations of the remarks made by their officials whether in Serbia or abroad, in interviews after the crime which according to the statement of the Imperial and Royal Government were hostile towards the Monarchy, as soon as the Imperial and Royal Government have communicated to them the passages in question in these remarks, and as soon as they have shown that the remarks were actually made by the said officials, although the Royal Government will itself take steps to collect evidence and proofs.

The Royal Government will inform the Imperial and Royal Government of the execution of the measures comprised under the above heads, in so far as this has not already been done by the present note, as soon as each measure has been ordered and carried out.

If the Imperial and Royal Government are not satisfied with this reply, the Serbian Government, considering that it is not to the common interest to precipitate the solution of this question, are ready, as always, to accept a pacific understanding, either by referring this question to the decision of the International Tribunal of The Hague, or to the Great Powers which took part in the drawing up of the declaration made by the Serbian Government on the 18th (31st) March, 1909.

Belgrade, July 12 (25), 1914.

Sir M. de Bunsen, British Ambassador at Vienna, to Sir Edward Grey.—(Received July 27.)

(Telegraphic.)   Vienna, July 26, 1914.

RUSSIAN Ambassador just returned from leave thinks that Austro-Hungarian Government are determined on war, and that it is impossible for Russia to remain indifferent. He does not propose to press for more time in the sense of your telegram of the 25th instant (last paragraph).

When the repetition of your telegram of the 26th instant to Paris arrived, I had the French and Russian Ambassadors both with me. They expressed great satisfaction with its contents, which I communicated to them. They doubted, however, whether the principle of Russia being an interested party entitled to have a say in the settlement of a purely Austro-Serbian dispute would be accepted by either the Austro-Hungarian or the German Government.

Instructions were also given to the Italian Ambassador to support the request of the Russian Government that the time limit should be postponed.

They arrived, however, too late for any useful action to be taken.

Sir M. de Bunsen, British Ambassador at Vienna, to Sir Edward Grey.—(Received July 27.)
(Telegraphic.)   Vienna, July 27, 1914.

I HAVE had conversations with all my colleagues representing the Great Powers. The impression left on my mind is that the Austro-Hungarian note was so drawn up as to make war inevitable; that the Austro-Hungarian Government are fully resolved to have war with Serbia; that they consider their position as a Great Power to be at stake; and that until punishment has been administered to Serbia it is unlikely that they will listen to proposals of mediation. This country has gone wild with joy at the prospect of war with Serbia, and its postponement or prevention would undoubtedly be a great disappointment.

I propose, subject to any special directions you desire to send me, to express to the Austrian Minister for Foreign Affairs the hope of His Majesty's Government that it may yet be possible to avoid war, and to ask his Excellency whether he cannot suggest a way out even now.

Sir F. Bertie, British Ambassador at Paris, to Sir Edward Grey.—(Received July 27.)
(Telegraphic.)   Paris, July 27, 1914.

YOUR proposal, as stated in your two telegrams of yesterday, is accepted by the French Government.

French Ambassador in London, who returns there this evening, has been instructed accordingly. Instructions have been sent to the French Ambassador at Berlin to concert with his British colleague as to the advisability of their speaking jointly to the German Government. Necessary instructions have also been sent to the French representatives at Belgrade, Vienna, and St. Petersburgh, but until it is known that the Germans have spoken at Vienna with some success, it would, in the opinion of the Ministry of Foreign Affairs, be dangerous for the French, Russian, and British Ambassadors to do so.

Sir E. Goschen, British Ambassador at Berlin, to Sir Edward Grey.—(Received July 27.)
(Telegraphic.)   Berlin, July 27, 1914.

YOUR telegram of 26th July.

Secretary of State says that conference you suggest would practically amount to a court of arbitration and could not, in his opinion, be called together except at the request of Austria and Russia. He could not therefore fall in with your suggestion, desirous though he was to co-operate for the maintenance of peace. I said I was sure that your idea had nothing to do with arbitration, but meant that representatives of the four nations not directly interested should discuss and suggest means for avoiding a dangerous situation. He maintained, however, that such a conference as you proposed was not practicable. He added that news he had just received from St.

Petersburgh showed that there was an intention on the part of M. de Sazonof to exchange views with Count Berchtold. He thought that this method of procedure might lead to a satisfactory result, and that it would be best, before doing anything else, to await outcome of the exchange of views between the Austrian and Russian Governments.

In the course of a short conversation Secretary of State said that as yet Austria was only partially mobilising but that if Russia mobilised against Germany latter would have to follow suit. I asked him what he meant by "mobilising against Germany." He said that if Russia only mobilised in south, Germany would not mobilise, but if she mobilised in north, Germany would have to do so too, and Russian system of mobilisation was so complicated that it might be difficult exactly to locate her mobilisation. Germany would therefore have to be very careful not to be taken by surprise.

Finally, Secretary of State said that news from St. Petersburgh had caused him to take more hopeful view of the general situation.

Sir G. Buchanan, British Ambassador at St. Petersburgh, to Sir Edward Grey.—(Received July 27.)
(Telegraphic.)   St. Petersburgh, July 27, 1914.

AUSTRIAN Ambassador tried, in a long conversation which he had yesterday with the Minister for Foreign Affairs, to explain away objectionable features of the recent action taken by the Austro-Hungarian

Government. Minister for Foreign Affairs pointed out that, although he perfectly understood Austria's motives, the ultimatum had been so drafted that it could not possibly be accepted as a whole by the Serbian Government. Although the demands were reasonable enough in some cases, others not only could not possibly be put into immediate execution seeing that they entailed revision of existing Serbian laws, but were, moreover, incompatible with Serbia's dignity as an independent State. It would be useless for Russia to offer her good offices at Belgrade, in view of the fact that she was the object of such suspicion in Austria. In order, however, to put an end to the present tension, he thought that England and Italy might be willing to collaborate with Austria. The Austrian Ambassador undertook to communicate his Excellency's remarks to his Government.

On the Minister for Foreign Affairs questioning me, I told him that I had correctly defined the attitude of His Majesty's Government in my conversation with him, which I reported in my telegram of the 24th instant. I added that you could not promise to do anything more, and that his Excellency was mistaken if he believed that the cause of peace could be promoted by our telling the German Government that they would have to deal with us as well as with Russia and France if they supported Austria by force of arms. Their attitude would merely be stiffened by such a menace, and we could only induce her to use her influence at Vienna to avert war by approaching her in the capacity of a friend who was anxious to preserve peace. His Excellency must not, if our efforts were to be successful, do anything to precipitate a conflict. In these circumstances I trusted that the Russian Government would defer mobilisation for as long as possible, and that troops would not be allowed to cross the frontier even when it was issued.

In reply the Minister for Foreign Affairs told me that until the issue of the Imperial ukase no effective steps towards mobilisation could be taken, and the Austro-Hungarian Government would profit by delay in order to complete her military preparations if it was deferred too long.

Sir G. Buchanan, British Ambassador at St. Petersburgh, to Sir Edward Grey.—(Received July 27.)
(Telegraphic.)   St. Petersburgh, July 27, 1914.

SINCE my conversation with the Minister for Foreign Affairs, as reported in my telegram of to-day, I understand that his Excellency has proposed that the modifications to be introduced into Austrian demands should be the subject of direct conversation between Vienna and St. Petersburgh.

Sir Edward Grey to Sir E. Goschen, British Ambassador at Berlin.
(Telegraphic.)   Foreign Office, July 27, 1914.

GERMAN Ambassador has informed me that German Government accept in principle mediation between Austria and Russia by the four Powers, reserving, of course, their right as an ally to help Austria if attacked. He has also been instructed to request me to use influence in St. Petersburgh to localise the war and to keep up the peace of Europe.

I have replied that the Serbian reply went farther than could have been expected to meet the Austrian demands. German Secretary of State has himself said that there were some things in the Austrian note that Serbia could hardly be expected to accept. I assumed that Serbian reply could not have gone as far as it did unless Russia had exercised conciliatory influence at Belgrade, and it was really at Vienna that moderating influence was now required. If Austria put the Serbian reply aside as being worth nothing and marched into Serbia, it meant that she was determined to crush Serbia at all costs, being reckless of the consequences that might be involved. Serbian reply should at least be treated as a basis for discussion and pause. I said German Government should urge this at Vienna.

I recalled what German Government had said as to the gravity of the situation if the war could not be localised, and observed that if Germany assisted Austria against Russia it would be because, without any reference to the merits of the dispute, Germany could not afford to see Austria crushed. Just so other issues might be raised that would supersede the dispute between Austria and Serbia, and would bring other Powers in, and the war would be the biggest ever known; but as long as Germany would work to keep the peace I would keep closely in touch. I repeated that after the Serbian reply it was at Vienna that some moderation must be urged.

Sir Edward Grey to Sir G. Buchanan, British Ambassador at St. Petersburgh.
(Telegraphic.)   Foreign Office, July 27, 1914.

SEE my telegram of to-day to Sir E. Goschen.

I have been told by the Russian Ambassador that in German and Austrian circles impression prevails that in any event we would stand aside. His Excellency deplored the effect that such an impression must produce.

This impression ought, as I have pointed out, to be dispelled by the orders we have given to the First Fleet, which is concentrated, as it happens, at Portland, not to disperse for manœuvre leave. But I explained to the Russian Ambassador that my reference to it must not be taken to mean that anything more than diplomatic action was promised.

We hear from German and Austrian sources that they believe Russia will take no action so long as Austria agrees not to take Serbian territory. I pointed this out, and added that it would be absurd if we were to appear more Serbian than the Russians in our dealings with the German and Austrian Governments.

THE AUSTRIAN RESPONSE

Sir E. Grey to Sir M. de Bunsen, British Ambassador at Vienna.
Sir,   Foreign Office, July 27, 1914.

COUNT MENSDORFF told me by instruction to-day that the Serbian Government had not accepted the demands which the Austrian Government were obliged to address to them in order to secure permanently the most vital Austrian interests. Serbia showed that she did not intend to abandon her subversive aims, tending towards continuous disorder in the Austrian frontier territories and their final disruption from the Austrian Monarchy. Very reluctantly, and against their wish, the Austrian Government were compelled to take more severe measures to enforce a fundamental change of the attitude of enmity pursued up to now by Serbia. As the British Government knew, the Austrian Government had for many years endeavoured to find a way to get on with their turbulent neighbour, though this had been made very difficult for them by the continuous provocations of Serbia. The Serajevo murder had made clear to everyone what appalling consequences the Serbian propaganda had already produced and what a permanent threat to Austria it involved. We would understand that the Austrian Government must consider that the moment had arrived to obtain, by means of the strongest pressure, guarantees for the definite suppression of the Serbian aspirations and for the security of peace and order on the south-eastern frontier of Austria. As the peaceable means to this effect were exhausted, the Austrian Government must at last appeal to force. They had not taken this decision without reluctance. Their action, which had no sort of aggressive tendency, could not be represented otherwise than as an act of self-defence. Also they thought that they would serve a European interest if they prevented Serbia from being henceforth an element of general unrest such as she had been for the last ten years. The high sense of justice of the British nation and of British statesmen could not blame the Austrian Government if the latter defended by the sword what was theirs, and cleared up their position with a country whose hostile policy had forced upon them for years measures so costly as to have gravely injured Austrian national prosperity. Finally, the Austrian Government, confiding in their amicable relations with us, felt that they could count on our sympathy in a fight that was forced on them, and on our assistance in localising the fight, if necessary.

Count Mensdorff added on his own account that, as long as Serbia was confronted with Turkey, Austria never took very severe measures because of her adherence to the policy of the free development of the Balkan States. Now that Serbia had doubled her territory and population without any Austrian interference, the repression of Serbian subversive aims was a matter of self-defence and self-preservation on Austria's part. He reiterated that Austria had no intention of taking Serbian territory or aggressive designs against Serbian territory.

I said that I could not understand the construction put by the Austrian Government upon the Serbian reply, and I told Count Mensdorff the substance of the conversation that I had had with the German Ambassador this morning about that reply.

Count Mensdorff admitted that, on paper, the Serbian reply might seem to be satisfactory; but the Serbians had refused the one thing—the co-operation of Austrian officials and police—which would be a real guarantee that in practice the Serbians would not carry on their subversive campaign against Austria.

I said that it seemed to me as if the Austrian Government believed that, even after the Serbian reply, they could make war upon Serbia anyhow, without risk of bringing Russia into the dispute. If they could make war on Serbia and at the same time satisfy Russia, well and good; but, if not, the consequences would be incalculable. I pointed out to him that I quoted this phrase from an expression of the views of the German Government. I feared that it would be expected in St. Petersburgh that the Serbian reply would diminish the tension, and now, when Russia found that there was increased tension, the situation would become increasingly serious. Already the effect on Europe was one of anxiety. I pointed out that our fleet was to have dispersed to-day, but we had felt unable to let it disperse. We should not think of calling up reserves at this moment, and there was no menace in what we had done about our fleet; but, owing to the possibility of a European conflagration, it was impossible for us to disperse our forces at this moment. I gave this as an illustration of the anxiety that was felt. It seemed to me that the Serbian reply already involved the greatest humiliation to Serbia that I had ever seen a country undergo, and it was very disappointing to me that the reply was treated by

the Austrian Government as if it were as unsatisfac-
tory as a blank negative.

I am, &c.

E. GREY.

*Sir Edward Grey to Sir R. Rodd, British Ambassador at
Rome.*

Sir,   Foreign Office, July 27, 1914.

THE Italian Ambassador informed Sir A. Nicolson
to-day that the Italian Minister for Foreign Affairs
agreed entirely with my proposal for a conference of
four to be held in London.

As regards the question of asking Russia, Austria-
Hungary, and Serbia to suspend military operations
pending the result of the conference, the Marquis di
San Giuliano would recommend the suggestion
warmly to the German Government, and would
enquire what procedure they would propose should
be followed at Vienna.

I am, &c.,

E. GREY.

TUESDAY JULY 28TH

Sir M. de Bunsen, British Ambassador at Vienna, to Sir Edward Grey.—(Received July 31.)

Sir,   Vienna, July 28, 1914.

I HAVE the honour to transmit to you herewith the text of the Austro-Hungarian note announcing the declaration of war against Serbia.

I have, &c.

MAURICE DE BUNSEN.

Copy of Note Verbale, Dated Vienna, July 28, 1914.

IN order to bring to an end the subversive intrigues originating from Belgrade and aimed at the territorial integrity of the Austro-Hungarian Monarchy, the Imperial and Royal Government has delivered to the Royal Serbian Government a note, dated July 23, 1914, in which a series of demands were formulated, for the acceptance of which a delay of forty-eight hours has been granted to the Royal Government. The Royal Serbian Government not having answered this note in a satisfactory manner, the Imperial and Royal Government are themselves compelled to see to the safeguarding of their rights and interests, and, with this object, to have recourse to force of arms.

Austria-Hungary, who has just addressed to Serbia a formal declaration, in conformity with article 1 of the convention of the 18th October, 1907, relative to the opening of hostilities, considers herself henceforward in a state of war with Serbia.

In bringing the above to notice of His Britannic Majesty's Embassy, the Ministry for Foreign Affairs has the honour to declare that Austria-Hungary will act during the hostilities in conformity with the terms of the Conventions of The Hague of the 18th October, 1907, as also with those of the Declaration of London of the 28th February, 1909, provided an analogous procedure is adopted by Serbia.

The embassy is requested to be so good as to communicate the present notification as soon as possible to the British Government.

Sir F. Bertie, British Ambassador at Paris, to Sir Edward Grey.—(Received July 28.)

Sir,   Paris, July 27, 1914.

I HAVE the honour to transmit to you herewith copy of a memorandum from the acting Minister for Foreign Affairs as to the steps to be taken to prevent an outbreak of hostilities between Austria-Hungary and Serbia.

I have, &c.

FRANCIS BERTIE.

Note Communicated to Sir F. Bertie by M. Bienvenu-Martin.

IN a note of the 25th of this month, his Excellency the British Ambassador informed the Government of the Republic that, in Sir E. Grey's opinion, the only possible way of assuring the maintenance of peace in case of the relations between Russia and Austria becoming more strained would be if the representatives of Great Britain, France, Germany, and Italy in Austria and Russia were to take joint action at Vienna and at St. Petersburg; and he expressed the wish to know if the Government of the Republic were disposed to welcome such a suggestion.

The Minister for Foreign Affairs *ad interim* has the honour to inform his Excellency Sir F. Bertie that he has requested M. Jules Cambon to concert with the British Ambassador in Germany and to support any representation which they may consider it advisable to make to the Berlin Cabinet.

In accordance with the desire expressed by the British Government and conveyed to them by Sir F.

Bertie in his note of the 26th of this month, the Government of the Republic have also authorised M. Paul Cambon to take part in the conference which Sir E. Grey has proposed with a view to discovering in consultation with himself and the German and Italian Ambassadors in London a means of settling the present difficulties.

The Government of the Republic is likewise ready to instruct the French representatives at St. Petersburgh, Vienna, and Belgrade to induce the Russian, Austrian, and Serbian Governments to abstain from all active military operations pending the results of this conference. He considers, however, that the chance of Sir E. Grey's proposal being successful depends essentially on the action which the Berlin Government would be willing to take at Vienna. Representations made to the Austrian-Hungarian Government for the purpose of bringing about a suspension of military operations would seem bound to fail unless the German Government do not beforehand exercise their influence on the Vienna Cabinet.

The President of the Council *ad interim* takes the opportunity, &c.

Paris, July 27, 1914.

Note Communicated by French Embassy, July 28, 1914.

THE Government of the Republic accept Sir Edward Grey's proposal in regard to intervention by Great Britain, France, Germany, and Italy with a view to avoiding active military operations on the frontiers

of Austria, Russia, and Serbia; and they have authorised M. P. Cambon to take part in the deliberations
of the four representatives at the meeting which is to
be held in London.

The French Ambassador in Berlin has received
instructions to consult first the British Ambassador in
Berlin, and then to support the action taken by the
latter in such manner and degree as may be considered appropriate.

M. Viviani is ready to send to the representatives
of France in Vienna, St. Petersburgh, and Belgrade
instructions in the sense suggested by the British
Government.

French Embassy, July 27, 1912.

*M. Sazonof, Russian Minister for Foreign Affairs, to Count
Benckendorff, Russian Ambassador in London.—
(Communicated by Count Benckendorff, July 28.)*
(Telegraphic.)   St. Petersburgh, July 27, 1914.

THE British Ambassador came to ascertain whether
we think it desirable that Great Britain should take
the initiative in convoking a conference in London of
the representatives of Great Britain, France, Germany,
and Italy to examine the possibility of a way out of
the present situation.

I replied to the Ambassador that I have begun
conversations   with   the   Austro-Hungarian
Ambassador under conditions which, I hope, may be
favourable. I have not, however, received as yet any
reply to the proposal made by me for revising the
note between the two Cabinets.

If direct explanations with the Vienna Cabinet were to prove impossible, I am ready to accept the British proposal, or any other proposal of a kind that would bring about a favourable solution of the conflict.

I wish, however, to put an end from this day forth to a misunderstanding which might arise from the answer given by the French Minister of Justice to the German Ambassador, regarding counsels of moderation to be given to the Imperial Cabinet.

M. Sazonof, Russian Minister for Foreign Affairs, to Count Benckendorff, Russian Ambassador in London.— (Communicated by Count Benckendorff, July 28, 1914.)
(Telegraphic.)   St. Petersburgh, July 15(28), 1914.

MY interviews with the German Ambassador confirm my impression that Germany is, if anything, in favour of the uncompromising attitude adopted by Austria.

The Berlin Cabinet, who could have prevented the whole of this crisis developing, appear to be exerting no influence on their ally.

The Ambassador considers that the Serbian reply is insufficient.

This attitude of the German Government is most alarming.

It seems to me that Great Britain is in a better position than any other Power to make another attempt at Berlin to induce the German Government to take the necessary action. There is no doubt that the key of the situation is to be found at Berlin.

Sir G. Buchanan, British Ambassador at St. Petersburgh, to Sir Edward Grey.—(Received July 28.)

(Telegraphic.)   St. Petersburgh, July 27, 1914.

WITH reference to my telegram of yesterday, I saw the Minister for Foreign Affairs this afternoon and found him very conciliatory and more optimistic.

He would, he said, use all his influence at Belgrade to induce the Serbian Government to go as far as possible in giving satisfaction to Austria, but her territorial integrity must be guaranteed and her rights as a sovereign State respected, so that she should not become Austria's vassal. He did not know whether Austria would accept friendly exchange of views which he had proposed, but, if she did, he wished to keep in close contact with the other Powers throughout the conversations that would ensue.

He again referred to the fact that the obligations undertaken by Serbia in 1908, alluded to in the Austrian ultimatum, were given to the Powers.

I asked if he had heard of your proposal with regard to conference of the four Powers, and on his replying in the affirmative, I told him confidentially of your instructions to me, and enquired whether instead of such a conference he would prefer a direct exchange of views, which he had proposed. The German Ambassador, to whom I had just spoken, had expressed his personal opinion that a direct exchange of views would be more agreeable to Austria-Hungary.

His Excellency said he was perfectly ready to

stand aside if the Powers accepted the proposal for a conference, but he trusted that you would keep in touch with the Russian Ambassador in the event of its taking place.

Sir M. de Bunsen, British Ambassador at Vienna, to Sir Edward Grey.—(Received July 28.)
(Telegraphic.)   Vienna, July 27, 1914.

THE Russian Ambassador had to-day a long and earnest conversation with Baron Macchio, the Under-Secretary of State for Foreign Affairs. He told him that, having just come back from St. Petersburgh, he was well acquainted with the views of the Russian Government and the state of Russian public opinion. He could assure him that if actual war broke out with Serbia it would be impossible to localise it, for Russia was not prepared to give way again, as she had done on previous occasions, and especially during the annexation crisis of 1909. He earnestly hoped that something would be done before Serbia was actually invaded. Baron Macchio replied that this would now be difficult, as a skirmish had already taken place on the Danube, in which the Serbians had been the aggressors. The Russian Ambassador said that he would do all he could to keep the Serbians quiet pending any discussions that might yet take place, and he told me that he would advise his Government to induce the Serbian Government to avoid any conflict as long as possible, and to fall back before an Austrian advance. Time so gained should suffice to enable a settlement to be

reached. He had just heard of a satisfactory conversation which the Russian Minister for Foreign Affairs
had yesterday with the Austrian Ambassador at St.
Petersburgh. The former had agreed that much of the
Austro-Hungarian note to Serbia had been perfectly
reasonable, and in fact they had practically reached an
understanding as to the guarantees which Serbia might
reasonably be asked to give to Austria-Hungary for her
future good behaviour. The Russian Ambassador
urged that the Austrian Ambassador at St. Petersburgh
should be furnished with full powers to continue discussion with the Russian Minister for Foreign Affairs,
who was very willing to advise Serbia to yield all that
could be fairly asked of her as an independent Power.
Baron Macchio promised to submit this suggestion to
the Minister for Foreign Affairs.

*Sir R. Rodd, British Ambassador at Rome, to Sir Edward
Grey.—(Received July 28.)*
(Telegraphic.)   Rome, July 27, 1914.

MINISTER for Foreign Affairs greatly doubts
whether Germany will be willing to invite Austria to
suspend military action pending the conference, but
he had hopes that military action may be practically
deferred by the fact of the conference meeting at
once. As at present informed, he sees no possibility of
Austria receding from any point laid down in her
note to Serbia, but he believes that if Serbia will even
now accept it Austria will be satisfied, and if she had
reason to think that such will be the advice of the

Powers, Austria may defer action. Serbia may be induced to accept note in its entirety on the advice of the four Powers invited to the conference, and this would enable her to say that she had yielded to Europe and not to Austria-Hungary alone.

Telegrams from Vienna to the press here stating that Austria is favourably impressed with the declarations of the Italian Government have, the Minister for Foreign Affairs assures me, no foundation. He said he has expressed no opinion to Austria with regard to the note. He assured me both before and after communication of the note, and again to-day, that Austrian Government have given him assurances that they demand no territorial sacrifices from Serbia.

Sir F. Bertie, British Ambassador at Paris, to Sir Edward Grey.—(Received July 28.)
(Telegraphic.)   Paris, July 28, 1914.

I COMMUNICATED to the Acting Minister for Foreign Affairs this afternoon the substance of your conversation with the German Ambassador, recorded in your telegram to Berlin of the 27th July.

His Excellency is grateful for the communication. He said that it confirms what he had heard of your attitude, and he feels confident that your observations to the German Ambassador will have a good effect in the interest of peace.

Sir F. Bertie, British Ambassador at Paris, to Sir Edward Grey.—(Received July 28.)
(Telegraphic.)   Paris, July 28, 1914.

I INFORMED the Acting Minister for Foreign Affairs to-day of your conversation with the Russian Ambassador, as recorded in your telegram of yesterday to St. Petersburgh.

He is grateful for the communication, and quite appreciates the impossibility for His Majesty's Government to declare themselves "solidaires" with Russia on a question between Austria and Serbia, which in its present condition is not one affecting England. He also sees that you cannot take up an attitude at Berlin and Vienna more Serbian than that attributed in German and Austrian sources to the Russian Government.

German Ambassador has stated that Austria would respect the integrity of Serbia, but when asked whether her independence also would be respected, he gave no assurance.

Sir E. Goschen, British Ambassador at Berlin, to Sir Edward Grey.—(Received July 28.)
(Telegraphic.)   Berlin, July 28, 1914.

SECRETARY of State spoke yesterday in the same sense as that reported in my telegram of yesterday to my French and Italian colleagues respecting your proposal. I discussed with my two colleagues this morning his reply, and we found that, while refusing the proposed conference, he had said to all of us that nevertheless he desired to work with us for the maintenance of general peace. We therefore deduced that if he is sincere in this wish he can only be objecting to the form of your proposal. Perhaps he himself could be induced to suggest lines on which he would find it possible to work with us.

Sir M. de Bunsen, British Ambassador at Vienna, to Sir Edward Grey.—(Received July 28.)
(Telegraphic.)   Vienna, July 28, 1914.

I SAW Minister for Foreign Affairs this morning.

His Excellency declared that Austria-Hungary cannot delay warlike proceedings against Serbia, and would have to decline any suggestion of negotiations on basis of Serbian reply.

Prestige of Dual Monarchy was engaged, and nothing could now prevent conflict.

Sir M. de Bunsen, British Ambassador at Vienna, to Sir Edward Grey.—(Received July 28.)
(Telegraphic.)   Vienna, July 28, 1914.

I SPOKE to Minister for Foreign Affairs to-day in the sense of your telegram of 27th July to Berlin. I avoided the word "mediation," but said that, as mentioned in your speech, which he had just read to me, you had hopes that conversations in London between the four Powers less interested might yet lead to an arrangement which Austro-Hungarian Government would accept as satisfactory and as rendering actual hostilities unnecessary. I added that you had regarded Serbian reply as having gone far to meet just demands of Austria-Hungary; that you thought it constituted a fair basis of discussion during which warlike operations might remain in abeyance, and that Austrian Ambassador in Berlin was speaking in this sense. Minister for Foreign Affairs said quietly, but firmly, that no discussion could be accepted on basis of Serbian note; that war would be declared to-day, and that well-known pacific character of Emperor, as well as, he might add, his own, might be accepted as a guarantee that war was both just and inevitable. This was a matter that must be settled directly between the two parties immediately concerned. I said that you would hear with regret that hostilities could not now be arrested, as you feared that they might lead to complications threatening the peace of Europe.

In taking leave of his Excellency, I begged him to believe that, if in the course of present grave crisis our point of view should sometimes differ from his, this would arise, not from want of sympathy with the many just complaints which Austria-Hungary had against Serbia, but from the fact that, whereas Austria-Hungary put first her quarrel with Serbia, you were anxious in the first instance for peace of Europe. I trusted this larger aspect of the question would appeal with equal force to his Excellency. He said he had it also in mind, but thought that Russia ought not to oppose operations like those impending, which did not aim at territorial aggrandisement and which could no longer be postponed.

Sir R. Rodd, British Ambassador at Rome, to Sir Edward Grey.—(Received July 28.)
(Telegraphic.)   Rome, July 28, 1914.

YOUR telegram of 25th July to Paris.

I have communicated substance to Minister for Foreign Affairs, who immediately telegraphed in precisely similar terms to Berlin and Vienna.

Sir R. Rodd, British Ambassador at Rome, to Sir Edward Grey—(Received July 28.)
(Telegraphic.)   Rome, July 28, 1914.

AT the request of the Minister for Foreign Affairs I submit the following to you:—

In a long conversation this morning Serbian Chargé d'Affaires had said he thought that if some explanations were given regarding mode in which Austrian agents would require to intervene under article 5 and article 6, Serbia might still accept the whole Austrian note.

As it was not to be anticipated that Austria would give such explanations to Serbia, they might be given to Powers engaged in discussions, who might then advise Serbia to accept without conditions.

The Austro-Hungarian Government had in the meantime published a long official explanation of grounds on which Serbian reply was considered inadequate. Minister for Foreign Affairs considered many points besides explanation—such as slight verbal difference in sentence regarding renunciation of propaganda—quite childish, but there was a passage which might prove useful in facilitating such a course as was considered practicable by the Serbian Chargé d'Affaires. It was stated that co-operation of Austrian agents in Serbia was to be only in investigation, not in judicial or administrative measures. Serbia was said to have wilfully misinterpreted this. He thought, therefore, that ground might be cleared here.

I only reproduce from memory, as I had not yet received text of Austrian declaration.

Minister impressed upon me, above all, his anxiety for the immediate beginning of discussion. A wide general latitude to accept at once every point or suggestion on which he could be in agreement with ourselves and Germany had been given to Italian Ambassador.

Mr. Crackanthorpe, British Chargé d'Affaires at Belgrade, to Sir Edward Grey.—(Received July 28.)
(Telegraphic.)   Nish, July 28, 1914.

I HAVE urged on the Serbian Government the greatest moderation pending efforts being made towards a peaceful solution.

Two Serbian steamers fired on and damaged, and two Serbian merchant-vessels have been captured by a Hungarian monitor at Orsova.

Mr. Crackanthorpe, British Chargé d'Affaires at Belgrade, to Sir Edward Grey.—(Received July 28.)
(Telegraphic.)   Nish, July 28, 1914.

TELEGRAM received here that war declared by Austria.

Sir Edward Grey to Sir E. Goschen, British Ambassador at Berlin.
(Telegraphic.)   Foreign Office, July 28, 1914.

EXPLANATION given in your telegram of the 27th July of what was my idea in proposing a conference is quite right. It would not be an arbitration, but a private and informal discussion to ascertain what suggestion could be made for a settlement. No suggestion would be put forward that had not previously been ascertained to be acceptable to Austria and Russia, with whom the mediating Powers could easily keep in touch through their respective allies.

But as long as there is a prospect of a direct exchange of views between Austria and Russia, I would suspend every other suggestion, as I entirely agree that it is the most preferable method of all.

I understand that the Russian Minister for Foreign Affairs has proposed a friendly exchange of views to the Austrian Government, and, if the latter accepts, it will no doubt relieve the tension and make the situation less critical.

It is very satisfactory to hear from the German Ambassador here that the German Government have taken action at Vienna in the sense of the conversation recorded in my telegram of yesterday to you.

Sir Edward Grey to Sir E. Goschen, British Ambassador at Berlin.
(Telegraphic.)   Foreign Office, July 28, 1914.

GERMAN Government, having accepted principle of mediation between Austria and Russia by the four Powers, if necessary, I am ready to propose that the German Secretary of State should suggest the lines on which this principle should be applied. I will, however, keep the idea in reserve until we see how the conversations between Austria and Russia progress.

Sir Edward Grey to Sir G. Buchanan, British Ambassador at St. Petersburgh.
(Telegraphic.)   Foreign Office, July 28, 1914.

IT is most satisfactory that there is a prospect of direct exchange of views between the Russian and Austrian Governments, as reported in your telegram of the 27th July.

I am ready to put forward any practical proposal that would facilitate this, but I am not quite clear as to what the Russian Minister for Foreign Affairs proposes the Ministers at Belgrade should do. Could he not first mention in an exchange of views with Austria his willingness to co-operate in some such scheme? It might then take more concrete shape.

WEDNESDAY JULY 29TH

Telegrams communicated by Count Benckendorff, Russian Ambassador in London, July 29, 1914.

(1.) Telegram from M. Sazonof to Russian Ambassador at Berlin, dated July 28, 1914

IN consequence of the declaration of war by Austria against Serbia, the Imperial Government will announce to-morrow (29th) the mobilisation in the military circonscriptions of Odessa, Kieff, Moscow, and Kazan. Please inform German Government, confirming the absence in Russia of any aggressive intention against Germany.

The Russian Ambassador at Vienna has not been recalled from his post.

(2.) Telegram to Count Benckendorff.

The Austrian declaration of war clearly puts an end to the idea of direct communications between Austria and Russia. Action by London Cabinet in order to set on foot mediation with a view to suspension of military operations of Austria against Serbia is now most urgent.

Unless military operations are stopped, mediation would only allow matters to drag on and give Austria time to crush Serbia.

Sir E. Goschen, British Ambassador at Berlin, to Sir Edward Grey.—(Received July 29.)
(Telegraphic.)   Berlin, July 28, 1914.

AT invitation of Imperial Chancellor, I called upon his Excellency this evening. He said that he wished me to tell you that he was most anxious that Germany should work together with England for maintenance of general peace, as they had done successfully in the last European crisis. He had not been able to accept your proposal for a conference of representatives of the Great Powers, because he did not think that it would be effective, and because such a conference would in his opinion have had appearance of an "Areopagus" consisting of two Powers of each group sitting in judgment upon the two remaining Powers; but his inability to accept proposed conference must not be regarded as militating against his strong desire for effective co-operation. You could be assured that he was doing his very best both at Vienna and St. Petersburgh to get the two Governments to discuss the situation directly with each other and in a friendly way. He had great hopes that such discussions would take place and lead to a satisfactory result, but if the news were true which he had just read in the papers, that Russia had mobilised fourteen army corps in the south, he thought situation was very serious, and he himself would be in a very difficult position, as in these circumstances it would be out of his power to continue to preach moderation at Vienna. He added that Austria, who as yet was only partially mobilising, would have to take similar measures, and if war were to result, Russia would be entirely responsible. I ventured to say that if Austria refused to take any notice of Serbian note, which, to my mind, gave way in nearly every point demanded by Austria, and which in any case offered a basis for discussion, surely a certain portion of responsibility would rest with her. His Excellency said that he did not wish to discuss Serbian note, but that Austria's standpoint, and in this he agreed, was that her quarrel with Serbia was a purely Austrian concern with which Russia had nothing to do. He reiterated his desire to co-operate with England and his intention to do his utmost to maintain general peace. "A war between the Great Powers must be avoided" were his last words.

Austrian colleague said to me to-day that a general war was most unlikely, as Russia neither wanted nor was in a position to make war. I think that that opinion is shared by many people here.

Sir G. Buchanan, British Ambassador at St. Petersburgh, to Sir Edward Grey.—(Received July 29.)
(Telegraphic.)   St. Petersburgh, July 28, 1914.

MINISTER for Foreign Affairs begged me to thank you for the language you had held to the German Ambassador, as reported in your telegram to Berlin, substance of which I communicated to his Excellency. He took a pessimistic view of the situation, having received the same disquieting news from Vienna as had reached. His Majesty's Government. I said it was important that we should know the real intentions of the Imperial Government, and asked him whether he would be satisfied with the assurances which the Austrian Ambassador had, I understood, been instructed to give in respect of Serbia's integrity and independence. I added that I was sure any arrangement for averting a European war would be welcomed by His Majesty's Government. In reply his Excellency stated that if Serbia were attacked Russia would not be satisfied with any engagement which Austria might take on these two points, and that order for mobilisation against Austria would be issued on the day that Austria crossed Serbian frontier.

I told the German Ambassador, who appealed to me to give moderating counsels to the Minister for

Foreign Affairs, that from the beginning I had not ceased to do so, and that the German Ambassador at Vienna should now in his turn use his restraining influence. I made it clear to his Excellency that, Russia being thoroughly in earnest, a general war could not be averted if Serbia were attacked by Austria.

As regards the suggestion of conference, the Ambassador had received no instructions, and before acting with me the French and Italian Ambassadors are still waiting for their final instructions.

Sir M. de Bunsen, British Ambassador at Vienna, to Sir Edward Grey.—(Received July 29.)
(Telegraphic.)   Vienna, July 28, 1914.

I HAVE received *note verbale* from Ministry for Foreign Affairs, stating that, the Serbian Government not having replied to note of 23rd July in a satisfactory manner, Imperial and Royal Government is compelled itself to provide for protection of its rights, and to have recourse for that object to force of arms. Austria-Hungary has addressed to Serbia formal declaration according to article 1 of convention of 18th October, 1907, relative to opening of hostilities, and considers herself from to-day in state of war with Serbia. Austria-Hungary will conform, provided Serbia does so, to stipulations of Hague conventions of 18th October, 1907, and to Declaration of London of 26th February, 1909.

Sir M. de Bunsen, British Ambassador at Vienna, to Sir Edward Grey.—(Received July 29.)

(Telegraphic.)   Vienna, July 28, 1914.

I AM informed by the Russian Ambassador that the Russian Government's suggestion has been declined by the Austro-Hungarian Government. The suggestion was to the effect that the means of settling the Austro-Serbian conflict should be discussed directly between Russian Minister for Foreign Affairs and the Austrian Ambassador at St. Petersburgh, who should be authorised accordingly.

The Russian Ambassador thinks that a conference in London of the less interested Powers, such as you have proposed, offers now the only prospect of preserving peace of Europe, and he is sure that the Russian Government will acquiesce willingly in your proposal. So long as opposing armies have not actually come in contact, all hope need not be abandoned.

Sir E. Goschen, British Ambassador at Berlin, to Sir Edward Grey.—(Received July 29.)

(Telegraphic.)   Berlin, July 29, 1914.

I WAS sent for again to-day by the Imperial Chancellor, who told me that he regretted to state that the Austro-Hungarian Government, to whom he had at once communicated your opinion, had answered that events had marched too rapidly and that it was therefore too late to act upon your suggestion that the Serbian reply might form the basis of discussion. His Excellency had, on receiving their reply, despatched a message to Vienna, in which he explained that, although a certain desire had, in his opinion, been shown in the Serbian reply to meet the demands of Austria, he understood entirely that, without some sure guarantees that Serbia would carry out in their entirety the demands made upon her, the Austro-Hungarian Government could not rest satisfied in view of their past experience. He had then gone on to say that the hostilities which were about to be undertaken against Serbia had presumably the exclusive object of securing such guarantees, seeing that the Austrian Government already assured the Russian Government that they had no territorial designs.

He advised the Austro-Hungarian Government, should this view be correct, to speak openly in this sense. The holding of such language would, he hoped, eliminate all possible misunderstandings.

As yet, he told me, he had not received a reply from Vienna.

From the fact that he had gone so far in the matter of giving advice at Vienna, his Excellency hoped that you would realise that he was sincerely doing all in his power to prevent danger of European complications.

The fact of his communicating this information to you was a proof of the confidence which he felt in you and evidence of his anxiety that you should know he was doing his best to support your efforts in the cause of general peace, efforts which he sincerely appreciated.

Sir E. Goschen, British Ambassador at Berlin, to Sir Edward Grey.—(Received July 29.)
(Telegraphic.)   Berlin, July 29, 1914.

I FOUND Secretary of State very depressed to-day. He reminded me that he had told me the other day that he had to be very careful in giving advice to Austria, as any idea that they were being pressed would be likely to cause them to precipitate matters and present a *fait accompli.* This had, in fact, now happened, and he was not sure that his communication of your suggestion that Serbia's reply offered a basis for discussion had not hastened declaration of war. He was much troubled by reports of mobilisation in Russia, and of certain military measures, which he did not specify, being taken in France. He subsequently spoke of these measures to my French colleague, who informed him that French Government had done nothing more than the German Government had done, namely, recalled officers on leave. His Excellency denied German Government had done this, but as a matter of fact it is true. My French colleague said to Under-Secretary of State, in course of conversation, that it seemed to him that when Austria had entered Serbia, and so satisfied her military prestige, the moment might then be favourable for four disinterested Powers to discuss situation and come forward with suggestions for preventing graver complications. Under-Secretary of

State seemed to think idea worthy of consideration, as he replied that would be a different matter from conference proposed by you.

Russian Ambassador returned to-day, and has informed Imperial Government that Russia is mobilising in four southern governments.

Sir Edward Grey to Sir E. Goschen, British Ambassador at Berlin.
(Telegraphic.)   Foreign Office, July 29, 1914.

I MUCH appreciate the language of Chancellor, as reported in your telegram of to-day. His Excellency may rely upon it that this country will continue, as heretofore, to strain every effort to secure peace and to avert the calamity we all fear. If he can induce Austria to satisfy Russia and to abstain from going so far as to come into collision with her, we shall all join in deep gratitude to his Excellency for having saved the peace of Europe.

Sir G. Buchanan, British Ambassador at St. Petersburgh, to Sir Edward Grey.—(Received July 29.)
(Telegraphic.)   St. Petersburgh, July 29, 1914.

PARTIAL mobilisation was ordered to-day.

I communicated the substance of your telegram of the 28th instant to Berlin to the Minister for Foreign Affairs in accordance with your instructions, and informed him confidentially of remarks as to mobilisation which the German Secretary of State had made to the British Ambassador at Berlin. This had already reached his Excellency from another source. The mobilisation, he explained, would only be directed against Austria.

Austrian Government had now definitely declined direct conversation between Vienna and St. Petersburgh. The Minister for Foreign Affairs said he had proposed such an exchange of views on advice of German Ambassador. He proposed, when informing German Ambassador of this refusal of Austria's, to urge that a return should be made to your proposal for a conference of four Ambassadors, or, at all events, for an exchange of views between the three Ambassadors less directly interested, yourself, and also the Austrian Ambassador if you thought it advisable. Any arrangement approved by France and England would be acceptable to him, and he did not care what form such conversations took. No time was to be lost, and the only way to avert war was for you to succeed in arriving, by mean of conversations with Ambassadors either collectively or individually, at some formula which Austria could be induced to accept. Throughout Russian Government had been perfectly frank and conciliatory, and had done all in their power to maintain peace. If their efforts to maintain peace failed, he trusted that it would be realised by the British public that it was not the fault of the Russian Government.

I asked him whether he would raise objections if the suggestion made in Rome telegram of the 27th July, which I mentioned to him, were carried out.

In reply his Excellency said that he would agree to anything arranged by the four Powers provided it was acceptable to Serbia; he could not, he said, be more Serbian than Serbia. Some supplementary statement or explanations would, however, have to be made in order to tone down the sharpness of the ultimatum.

Minister for Foreign Affairs said that proposal referred to in your telegram of the 28th instant was one of secondary importance. Under altered circumstances of situation he did not attach weight to it. Further, the German Ambassador had informed his Excellency, so the latter told me, that his Government were continuing at Vienna to exert friendly influence. I fear that the German Ambassador will not help to smooth matters over, if he uses to his own Government the same language as he did to me to-day. He accused the Russian Government of endangering the peace of Europe by their mobilisation, and said, when I referred to all that had been recently done by Austria, that he could not discuss such matters. I called his attention to the fact that Austrian consuls had warned all Austrian subjects liable to military service to join the colours, that Austria had already partially mobilised, and had now declared war on Serbia. From what had passed during the Balkan crisis she knew that this act was one which it was impossible without humiliation for Russia to submit to. Had not Russia by mobilising shown that she was in earnest, Austria would have traded on Russia's desire for peace, and would have believed that she could go to any lengths. Minister for Foreign

Affairs had given me to understand that Russia would not precipitate war by crossing frontier immediately, and a week or more would, in any case, elapse before mobilisation was completed. In order to find an issue out of a dangerous situation it was necessary that we should in the meanwhile all work together.

Sir M. de Bunsen, British Ambassador at Vienna, to Sir Edward Grey.—(Received July 29.)
(Telegraphic.)   Vienna, July 29, 1914.

THERE is at present no step which we could usefully take to stop war with Serbia, to which Austro-Hungarian Government are now fully committed by the Emperor's appeal to his people which has been published this morning, and by the declaration of war. French and Italian Ambassadors agree with me in this view. If the Austro-Hungarian Government would convert into a binding engagement to Europe the declaration which has been made at St. Petersburgh to the effect that she desires neither to destroy the independence of Serbia nor to acquire Serbian territory, the Italian Ambassador thinks that Russia might be induced to remain quiet. This, however, the Italian Ambassador is convinced the Austrian Government would refuse to do.

Sir R. Rodd, British Ambassador at Rome, to Sir Edward Grey.—(Received July 29.)
(Telegraphic.)   Rome, July 29, 1914.

IN your telegram of the 27th instant to Berlin, German Ambassador was reported to have accepted in principle the idea of a conference. This is in contradiction with the telegram of the 27th instant from Berlin.

Information received by the Italian Government from Berlin shows that German view is correctly represented in Sir E. Goschen's telegram of the 27th July, but what creates difficulty is rather the "conference," so the Minister for Foreign Affairs understands, than the principle. He is going to urge, in a telegram which he is sending to Berlin to-night, adherence to the idea of an exchange of views in London. He suggests that the German Secretary of State might propose a formula acceptable to his Government. Minister for Foreign Affairs is of opinion that this exchange of views would keep the door open if direct communication between Vienna and St. Petersburgh fails to have any result. He thinks that this exchange of views might be concomitant with such direct communication.

The German Government are also being informed that the Italian Government would not be pardoned by public opinion here unless they had taken every possible step so as to avoid war. He is urging that the German Government must lend their co-operation in this.

He added that there seemed to be a difficulty in making Germany believe that Russia was in earnest. As Germany, however, was really anxious for good relations with ourselves, if she believed that Great

Britain would act with Russia and France he thought it would have a great effect.

Even should it prove impossible to induce Germany to take part, he would still advocate that England and Italy, each as representing one group, should continue to exchange views.

Sir Edward Grey to Sir R. Rodd, British Ambassador at Rome.
(Telegraphic.)   Foreign Office, July 29, 1914.

WITH reference to your telegram of yesterday.

It is impossible for me to initiate discussions with Ambassadors here, as I understand from Austrian Minister for Foreign Affairs that Austria will not accept any discussion on basis of Serbian note, and the inference of all I have heard from Vienna and Berlin is that Austria will not accept any form of mediation by the Powers as between Austria and Serbia. Italian Minister for Foreign Affairs must therefore speak at Berlin and Vienna. I shall be glad if a favourable reception is given to any suggestions he can make there.

Mr. Beaumont, British Chargé d'Affaires at Constantinople, to Sir Edward Grey.—(Received July 29.)
(Telegraphic.)   Constantinople, July 29, 1914.

I UNDERSTAND that the designs of Austria may extend considerably beyond the sanjak and a punitive occupation of Serbian territory. I gathered this from a remark let fall by the Austrian Ambassador here, who spoke of the deplorable economic situation of Salonica under Greek administration and of the assistance on which the Austrian army could count from Mussulman population discontented with Serbian rule.

Mr. Crackanthorpe, British Chargé d'Affaires at Belgrade, to Sir Edward Grey.—(Received July 29.)
(Telegraphic.)   Nish, July 29, 1914.

I HAVE been requested by Prime Minister to convey to you expression of his deep gratitude for the statement which you made on the 27th instant in the House of Commons.

Sir Edward Grey to Sir E. Goschen, British Ambassador at Berlin.
(Telegraphic.)   Foreign Office, July 29, 1914.

THE German Ambassador has been instructed by the German Chancellor to inform me that he is endeavouring to mediate between Vienna and St. Petersburgh, and he hopes with good success. Austria and Russia seem to be in constant touch, and he is endeavouring to make Vienna explain in a satisfactory form at St. Petersburgh the scope and extension of Austrian proceedings in Serbia. I told the German Ambassador that an agreement arrived at direct between Austria and Russia would be the best possible solution. I would press no proposal as long as there was a prospect of that, but my information this morning was that the Austrian Government have declined the suggestion of the Russian Government that the Austrian Ambassador at St. Petersburgh should be authorised to discuss directly with the Russian Minister for Foreign Affairs the means of settling the Austro-Serbian conflict. The press correspondents at St. Petersburgh had been told that Russian Government would mobilise. The German Government had said that they were favourable in principle to mediation between Russia and Austria if necessary. They seemed to think the particular method of conference, consultation or discussion, or even conversations *à quatre* in London too formal a method. I urged that the German Government should suggest any method by which the influence of the four Powers could be used together to prevent war between Austria and Russia. France agreed, Italy agreed. The whole idea of mediation or mediating influence was ready to be put into operation by any method that Germany could suggest if mine was not acceptable. In fact mediation was ready to come into operation by any method that Germany thought possible if only Germany would "press the button" in the interests of peace.

Sir E. Goschen, British Ambassador at Berlin, to Sir Edward Grey.—(Received July 29.)
(Telegraphic.)   Berlin, July 29, 1914.

I WAS asked to call upon the Chancellor to-night. His Excellency had just returned from Potsdam.

He said that should Austria be attacked by Russia a European conflagration might, he feared, become inevitable, owing to Germany's obligations as Austria's ally, in spite of his continued efforts to maintain peace. He then proceeded to make the following strong bid for British neutrality. He said that it was clear, so far as he was able to judge the main principle which governed British policy, that Great Britain would never stand by and allow France to be crushed in any conflict there might be. That, however, was not the object at which Germany aimed. Provided that neutrality of Great Britain were certain, every assurance would be given to the British Government that the Imperial Government aimed at no territorial acquisitions at the expense of France should they prove victorious in any war that might ensue.

I questioned his Excellency about the French colonies, and he said that he was unable to give a similar undertaking in that respect. As regards Holland, however, his Excellency said that so long as Germany's adversaries respected the integrity and neutrality of the Netherlands. Germany was ready to give His Majesty's Government an assurance that she would do likewise. It depended upon the action of France what operations Germany might be forced to enter upon in Belgium, but when the war was over, Belgian integrity would be respected if she had not sided against Germany.

His Excellency ended by saying that ever since he had been Chancellor the object of his policy had been, as you were aware, to bring about an under-

standing with England; he trusted that these assurances might form the basis of that understanding
which he so much desired. He had in mind a general
neutrality agreement between England and Germany,
though it was of course at the present moment too
early to discuss details, and an assurance of British
neutrality in the conflict which present crisis might
possibly produce, would enable him to look forward
to realisation of his desire.

In reply to his Excellency's enquiry how I
thought his request would appeal to you, I said that I
did not think it probable that at this stage of events
you would care to bind yourself to any course of
action and that I was of opinion that you would
desire to retain full liberty.

Our conversation upon this subject having come
to an end, I communicated the contents of your
telegram of to-day to his Excellency, who expressed
his best thanks to you.

*Sir R. Rodd, British Ambassador at Rome, to Sir Edward
Grey.—(Received July 29.)*
(Telegraphic.)   Rome, July 29, 1914.

MINISTER for Foreign Affairs thinks that moment
is past for any further discussions on basis of Serbian
note, in view of communication made to-day by
Russia at Berlin regarding partial mobilisation. The
utmost he now hopes for is that Germany may use
her influence at Vienna to prevent or moderate any
further demands on Serbia.

Sir Edward Grey to Sir F. Bertie, British Ambassador at Paris.

Sir,   Foreign Office, July 29, 1914.

AFTER telling M. Cambon to-day how grave the situation seemed to be, I told him that I meant to tell the German Ambassador to-day that he must not be misled by the friendly tone of our conversations into any sense of false security that we should stand aside if all the efforts to preserve the peace, which we were now making in common with Germany, failed. But I went on to say to M. Cambon that I thought it necessary to tell him also that public opinion here approached the present difficulty from a quite different point of view from that taken during the difficulty as to Morocco a few years ago. In the case of Morocco the dispute was one in which France was primarily interested, and in which it appeared that Germany, in an attempt to crush France, was fastening a quarrel on France on a question that was the subject of a special agreement between France and us. In the present case the dispute between Austria and Serbia was not one in which we felt called to take a hand. Even if the question became one between Austria and Russia we should not feel called upon to take a hand in it. It would then be a question of the supremacy of Teuton or Slav—a struggle for supremacy in the Balkans; and our idea had always been to avoid being drawn into a war over a Balkan question. If Germany became involved and France became involved, we had not made up our minds what we should do; it was a case that we should have to consider. France would then have been drawn into a quarrel which was not hers, but in which, owing to her alliance, her honour and interest obliged her to engage. We were free from engagements, and we should have to decide what British interests required us to do. I thought it necessary to say that, because, as he knew, we were taking all precautions with regard to our fleet, and I was about to warn Prince Lichnowsky not to count on our standing aside, but it would not be fair that I should let M. Cambon be misled into supposing that this meant that we had decided what to do in a contingency that I still hoped might not arise.

M. Cambon said that I had explained the situation very clearly. He understood it to be that in a Balkan quarrel, and in a struggle for supremacy between Teuton and Slav we should not feel called to intervene; should other issues be raised, and Germany and France become involved, so that the question became one of the hegemony of Europe, we should then decide what it was necessary for us to do. He seemed quite prepared for this announcement, and made no criticism upon it.

He said French opinion was calm, but decided. He anticipated a demand from Germany that France would be neutral while Germany attacked Russia. This assurance France, of course, could not give; she was bound to help Russia if Russia was attacked.

I am, &c.,

E. GREY.

Sir Edward Grey to Sir E. Goschen, British Ambassador at Berlin.

Sir,   Foreign Office, July 29, 1914

I TOLD the German Ambassador this afternoon of the information that I had received, that Russia had informed Germany respecting her mobilisation. I also told him of the communication made by Count Benckendorff, that the Austrian declaration of war manifestly rendered vain any direct conversations between Russia and Austria. I said that the hope built upon those direct conversations by the German Government yesterday had disappeared to-day. To-day the German Chancellor was working in the interest of mediation in Vienna and St. Petersburgh. If he suc-ceeded, well and good. If not, it was more important than ever that Germany should take up what I had suggested to the German Ambassador this morning, and propose some method by which the four Powers should be able to work together to keep the peace of Europe. I pointed out, however, that the Russian Government, while desirous of mediation, regarded it as a condition that the military operations against Serbia should be suspended, as otherwise a mediation would only drag on matters, and give Austria time to crush Serbia. It was, of course, too late for all military operations against Serbia to be suspended. In a short time, I supposed, the Austrian forces would be in Belgrade, and in occupation of some Serbian terri-tory. But even then it might be possible to bring some mediation into existence, if Austria, while saying that she must hold the occupied territory until she had complete satisfaction from Serbia, stated that she would not advance further, pending an effort of the Powers to mediate between her and Russia.

The German Ambassador said that he had already telegraphed to Berlin what I had said to him this morning.

I am, &c.,

E. GREY.

Sir Edward Grey to Sir E. Goschen, British Ambassador at Berlin.

Sir,   Foreign Office, July 29, 1914.

AFTER speaking to the German Ambassador this afternoon about the European situation, I said that I wished to say to him, in a quite private and friendly way, something that was on my mind. The situation was very grave. While it was restricted to the issues at present actually involved we had no thought of interfering in it. But if Germany became involved in it, and then France, the issue might be so great that it would involve all European interests; and I did not wish him to be misled by the friendly tone of our conversation—which I hoped would continue—into thinking that we should stand aside.

He said that he quite understood this, but he asked whether I meant that we should, under certain circumstances, intervene?

I replied that I did not wish to say that, or to use

anything that was like a threat or an attempt to apply pressure by saying that, if things became worse, we should intervene. There would be no question of our intervening if Germany was not involved, or even if France was not involved. But we knew very well, that if the issue did become such that we thought British interests required us to intervene, we must intervene at once, and the decision would have to be very rapid, just as the decisions of other Powers had to be. I hoped that the friendly tone of our conversations would continue as at present, and that I should be able to keep as closely in touch with the German Government in working for peace. But if we failed in our efforts to keep the peace, and if the issue spread so that it involved practically every European interest, I did not wish to be open to any reproach from him that the friendly tone of all our conversations had misled him or his Government into supposing that we should not take action, and to the reproach that, if they had not been so misled, the course of things might have been different.

The German Ambassador took no exception to what I had said; indeed, he told me that it accorded with what he had already given in Berlin as his view of the situation.

I am, &c.

E. GREY.

Sir Edward Grey to Sir E. Goschen, British Ambassador at Berlin.

Sir,   Foreign Office, July 29, 1914.

IN addition to what passed with the German Ambassador this morning, as recorded in my telegram of the 29th July to your Excellency, I gave the Ambassador a copy of Sir Rennell Rodd's telegram of the 28th July and of my reply to it. I said I had begun to doubt whether even a complete acceptance of the Austrian demands by Serbia would now satisfy Austria. But there appeared, from what the Marquis di San Giuliano had said, to be a method by which, if the Powers were allowed to have any say in the matter, they might bring about complete satisfaction for Austria, if only the latter would give them an opportunity. I could, however, make no proposal, for the reasons I have given in my telegram to you, and could only give what the Italian Minister for Foreign Affairs had said to the German Ambassador for information, as long as it was understood that Austria would accept no discussion with the Powers over her dispute with Serbia. As to mediation between Austria and Russia, I said it could not take the form simply of urging Russia to stand on one side while Austria had a free hand to go to any length she pleased. That would not be mediation, it would simply be putting pressure upon Russia in the interests of Austria. The German Ambassador said the view of the German Government was that Austria could not by force be humiliated, and could not abdicate her position as a Great Power. I said I entirely agreed, but it was not a question of humiliating Austria, it was a question of how far Austria meant to push the humiliation of others. There must, of course, be some humiliation of

Serbia, but Austria might press things so far as to involve the humiliation of Russia.

The German Ambassador said that Austria would not take Serbian territory, as to which I observed that, by taking territory while leaving nominal Serbian independence, Austria might turn Serbia practically into a vassal State, and this would affect the whole position of Russia in the Balkans.

I observed that when there was danger of European conflict it was impossible to say who would not be drawn into it. Even the Netherlands apparently were taking precautions.

The German Ambassador said emphatically that some means must be found of preserving the peace of Europe.

I am, &c.

E. GREY.

Sir Edward Grey to Sir M. de Bunsen, British Ambassador at Vienna.

Sir,   Foreign Office, July 29, 1914.

THE Austrian Ambassador told me to-day he had ready a long memorandum, which he proposed to leave, and which he said gave an account of the conduct of Serbia towards Austria, and an explanation of how necessary the Austrian action was.

I said that I did not wish to discuss the merits of the question between Austria and Serbia. The news to-day seemed to me very bad for the peace of

Europe. The Powers were not allowed to help in getting satisfaction for Austria, which they might get if they were given an opportunity, and European peace was at stake.

Count Mensdorff said that the war with Serbia must proceed. Austria could not continue to be exposed to the necessity of mobilising again and again, as she had been obliged to do in recent years. She had no idea of territorial aggrandisement, and all she wished was to make sure that her interests were safeguarded.

I said that it would be quite possible, without nominally interfering with the independence of Serbia or taking away any of her territory, to turn her into a sort of vassal State.

Count Mensdorff deprecated this.

In reply to some further remarks of mine, as to the effect that the Austrian action might have upon the Russian position in the Balkans, he said that, before the Balkan war, Serbia had always been regarded as being in the Austrian sphere of influence. I am, &c.

E. GREY.

Sir Edward Grey to Sir R. Rodd, British Ambassador at Rome.

Sir,   Foreign Office, July 29, 1914.

THE Italian Ambassador made to me to-day a communication from the Marquis di San Giuliano suggesting that the German objections to the mediation of the four Powers, a mediation that was strongly favoured by Italy, might be removed by some change in the form of procedure.

I said that I had already anticipated this by asking the German Government to suggest any form of procedure under which the idea of mediation between Austria and Russia, already accepted by the German Government in principle, could be applied.

I am, &c.

E. GREY.

Telegrams Communicated by Count Benckendorff, Russian Ambassador in London, July 30, 1914.

(1.)

Russian Ambassador at Vienna to M. Sazonof.

(Telegraphic.)   Vienna, July 15 (28), 1914.

I SPOKE to Count Berchtold to-day in the sense of your Excellency's instructions. I brought to his notice, in the most friendly manner, how desirable it was to find a solution which, while consolidating good relations between Austria-Hungary and Russia, would give to the Austro-Hungarian Monarchy genuine guarantees for its future relations with Serbia.

I drew Count Berchtold's attention to all the dangers to the peace of Europe which would be involved by an armed conflict between Austria-Hungary and Serbia.

Count Berchtold replied that he was well aware of the gravity of the situation and of the advantages of a frank explanation with the St. Petersburgh Cabinet. He told me that, on the other hand, the Austro-Hungarian Government, who had only decided much against their will on the energetic measures which they had taken against Serbia, could no longer recede, nor enter into any discussion about the terms of the Austro-Hungarian note.

Count Berchtold added that the crisis had become so acute, and that public opinion had risen to such a pitch of excitement, that the Government, even if they wished it, could no longer consent to such a course. This was all the more impossible, he said, inasmuch as the Serbian reply itself furnished proof of the insincerity of Serbia's promises for the future.

(2.)

M. Sazonof, Russian Minister for Foreign Affairs, to Count Benckendorff, Russian Ambassador in London.

(Telegraphic.)   St. Petersburgh, July 16 (29), 1914.

THE German Ambassador informs me, in the name of the Chancellor, that Germany has not ceased to exercise a moderating influence at Vienna, and that she will continue to do so even after the declaration of war. Up to this morning there had been no news that the Austrian army has crossed the Serbian frontier. I have begged the Ambassador to express my thanks to the Chancellor for the friendly tenour of this communication. I have informed him of the military measures taken by Russia, none of which, I told him, were directed against Germany; I added that neither should they be taken as aggressive measures against Austria-Hungary, their explanation being the mobilisation of the greater part of the Austro-Hungarian army.

The Ambassador said that he was in favour of direct explanations between the Austrian Government and ourselves, and I replied that I, too, was quite willing, provided that the advice of the German Government, to which he had referred, found an echo at Vienna.

I said at the same time that we were quite ready to accept the proposal for a conference of the four Powers, a proposal with which, apparently, Germany was not in entire sympathy.

I told him that, in my opinion, the best manner of turning to account the most suitable methods of finding a peaceful solution would be by arranging for parallel discussions to be carried on by a conference of the four Powers—Germany, France, Great Britain, and Italy—and by a direct exchange of views between Austria-Hungary and Russia on much the same lines as occurred during the most critical moments of last year's crisis.

I told the Ambassador that, after the concessions which had been made by Serbia, it should not be very difficult to find a compromise to settle the other questions which remained outstanding, provided that Austria showed some good-will and that all the Powers used their entire influence in the direction of conciliation.

(3.)

M. Sazonof, Russian Minister for Foreign Affairs, to Count Benckendorff, Russian Ambassador in London.

(Telegraphic.)   St. Petersburgh, July 16 (29), 1914.

AT the time of my interview with the German Ambassador, dealt with in my preceding telegram, I had not yet received M. Schébéko's telegram of the 15th (28th) July.

The contents of this telegram constitute a refusal of the Vienna Cabinet to agree to a direct exchange of views with the Imperial Government.

From now on, nothing remains for us to do but to rely entirely on the British Government to take the initiative in any steps which they may consider advisable.

Sir M. de Bunsen, British Ambassador at Vienna, to Sir Edward Grey.—(Received July 30.)

(Telegraphic.)   Vienna, July 29, 1914.

I LEARN that mobilisation of Russian corps destined to carry out operations on Austrian frontier has been ordered. My informant is Russian Ambassador. Ministry for Foreign Affairs here has realised, though somewhat late in the day, that Russia will not remain indifferent in present crisis. I believe that the news of Russian mobilisation will not be a surprise to the Ministry, but so far it is not generally known in Vienna this evening. Unless mediation, which German Government declared themselves ready to offer in concert with three other Great Powers not immediately interested in the Austro-Serbian dispute, be brought to bear forthwith, irrevocable steps may be taken in present temper of this country. German Ambassador feigns surprise that Serbian affairs should be of such interest to Russia. Both my Russian and French colleagues have spoken to him to-day. Russian Ambassador expressed the hope that it might still be possible to arrange matters, and explained that it was impossible for Russia to do otherwise than take an interest in the present dispute. Russia, he said, had done what she could already at Belgrade to induce Serbian Government to meet principal Austrian demands in a favourable spirit; if approached in a proper manner, he thought she would probably go still further in this direction. But she was justly offended at having been completely ignored, and she could not consent to be excluded from the settlement. German Ambassador said that if proposals were put forward which opened any prospect of possible acceptance by both sides, he personally thought that Germany might consent to act as mediator in concert with the three other Powers.

I gather from what Russian Ambassador said to me that he is much afraid of the effect that any serious engagement may have upon Russian public opinion. I gathered, however, that Russia would go a long way to meet Austrian demands on Serbia.

THURSDAY JULY 30TH

*Sir M. de Bunsen, British Ambassador at Vienna, to Sir
Edward Grey.—(Received July 30.)*
(Telegraphic.)   Vienna, July 30, 1914.

RUSSIAN Ambassador hopes that Russian mobilisation will be regarded by Austria as what it is, viz., a
clear intimation that Russia must be consulted
regarding the fate of Serbia, but he does not know
how the Austrian Government are taking it. He says
that Russia must have an assurance that Serbia will
not be crushed, but she would understand that
Austria-Hungary is compelled to exact from Serbia

measures which will secure her Slav provinces from the continuance of hostile propaganda from Serbian territory.

The French Ambassador hears from Berlin that the German Ambassador at Vienna is instructed to speak seriously to the Austro-Hungarian Government against acting in a manner calculated to provoke a European war.

Unfortunately the German Ambassador is himself so identified with extreme anti-Russian and anti-Serbian feeling prevalent in Vienna that he is unlikely to plead the cause of peace with entire sincerity.

Although I am not able to verify it, I have private information that the German Ambassador knew the text of the Austrian ultimatum to Serbia before it was despatched and telegraphed it to the German Emperor. I know from the German Ambassador himself that he endorses every line of it.

Sir M. de Bunsen, British Ambassador at Vienna, to Sir Edward Grey.—(Received July 30.)
(Telegraphic.)   Vienna, July 30, 1914.

THE Russian Ambassador gave the French Ambassador and myself this afternoon at the French Embassy, where I happened to be, an account of his interivew with the Minister for Foreign Affairs, which he said was quite friendly. The Minister for Foreign Affairs had told him that as Russia had mobilised, Austria must, of course, do the same. This, however, should not be regarded as a threat, but merely as the adoption of military precautions similar to those which had been taken across the frontier. He said he had no objection to the Russian Minister for Foreign Affairs and the Austrian Ambassador at St. Petersburgh continuing their conversations, although he did not say that they could be resumed on the basis of the Serbian reply.

On the whole, the Russian Ambassador is not dissatisfied. He had begun to make his preparations for his departure on the strength of a rumour that Austria would declare war in reply to mobilisation. He now hopes that something may yet be done to prevent war with Austria.

Sir G. Buchanan, British Ambassador at St. Petersburgh, to Sir Edward Grey.—(Received July 30.)

(Telegraphic.)   St. Petersburgh, July 30, 1914.

FRENCH Ambassador and I visited Minister for Foreign Affairs this morning. His Excellency said that German Ambassador had told him yesterday after-noon that German Government were willing to guarantee that Serbian integrity would be respected by Austria. To this he had replied that this might be so, but nevertheless Serbia would become an Austrian vassal, just as, in similar circumstances, Bokhara had become a Russian vassal. There would be a revolution in Russia if she were to tolerate such a state of affairs.

M. Sazonof told us that absolute proof was in possession of Russian Government that Germany was making military and naval preparations against

Russia—more particularly in the direction of the Gulf of Finland.

German Ambassador had a second interview with Minister for Foreign Affairs at 2 A.M., when former completely broke down on seeing that war was inevitable. He appealed to M. Sazonof to make some suggestion which he could telegraph to German Government as a last hope. M. Sazonof accordingly drew up and handed to German Ambassador a formula in French, of which following is translation:—

"If Austria, recognising that her conflict with Serbia has assumed character of question of European interest, declares herself ready to eliminate from her ultimatum points which violate principle of sovereignty of Serbia, Russia engages to stop all military preparations."

Preparations for general mobilisation will be proceeded with if this proposal is rejected by Austria, and inevitable result will be a European war. Excitement here has reached such a pitch that, if Austria refuses to make a concession, Russia cannot hold back, and now that she knows that Germany is arming, she can hardly postpone, for strategical reasons, coverting partial into general mobilisation.

Sir E. Goschen, British Ambassador at Berlin, to Sir Edward Grey.—(Received July 30.)

(Telegraphic.)   Berlin, July 30, 1914.

SECRETARY of State informs me that immediately on receipt of Prince Lichnowsky's telegram recording his last conversation with you he asked Austro-

Hungarian Government whether they would be willing to accept mediation on basis of occupation by Austrian troops of Belgrade or some other point and issue their conditions from here. He has up till now received no reply, but he fears Russian mobilisation against Austria will have increased difficulties, as Austria-Hungary, who has as yet only mobilised against Serbia, will probably find it necessary also against Russia. Secretary of State says if you can succeed in getting Russia to agree to above basis for an arrangement and in persuading her in the meantime to take no steps which might be regarded as an act of aggression against Austria he still sees some chance that European peace may be preserved.

He begged me to impress on you difficulty of Germany's position in view of Russian mobilisation and military measures which he hears are being taken in France. Beyond recall of officers on leave—a measure which had been officially taken after, and not before, visit of French ambassador yesterday—Imperial Government had done nothing special in way of military preparations. Something, however, would have soon to be done, for it might be too late, and when they mobilised they would have to mobilise on three sides. He regretted this, as he knew France did not desire war, but it would be a military necessity.

His Excellency added that telegram received from Prince Lichnowsky last night contains matter which he had heard with regret, but not exactly with surprise, and at all events he thoroughly appreciated frankness and loyalty with which you had spoken.

He also told me that this telegram had only
reached Berlin very late last night; had it been
received earlier Chancellor would, of course, not have
spoken to me in the way he had done.

*Sir F. Bertie, British Ambassador at Paris, to Sir Edward
Grey.—(Received July 30.)*
(Telegraphic.)   Paris, July 30, 1914.

PRESIDENT of the Republic tells me that the
Russian Government have been informed by the
German Government that unless Russia stops her
mobilisation Germany would mobilise. But a further
report, since received from St. Petersburgh, states that
the German communication had been modified, and
was now a request to be informed on what conditions
Russia would consent to demobilisation. The answer
given is that she agrees to do so on condition that
Austria-Hungary gives an assurance that she will
respect the sovereignty of Serbia and submit certain
of the demands of the Austrian note, which Serbia has
not accepted, to an international discussion.

President thinks that these conditions will not be
accepted by Austria. He is convinced that peace
between the Powers in the hands of Great Britain. If
His Majesty's Government announced that England
would come to the aid of France in the event of a
conflict between France and Germany as a result of
the present differences between Austria and Serbia,
there would be no war, for Germany would at once
modify her attitude.

I explained to him how difficult it would be for His Majesty's Government to make such an announcement, but he said that he must maintain that it would be in the interests of peace. France, he said, is pacific. She does not desire war, and all that she has done at present is to make preparations for mobilisation so as not to be taken unawares. The French Government will keep His Majesty's Government informed of everything that may be done in that way. They have reliable information that the German troops are concentrated round Thionville and Metz ready for war. If there were a general war on the Continent it would inevitably draw England into it for the protection of her vital interests. A declaration now of her intention to support France, whose desire it is that peace should be maintained, would almost certainly prevent Germany from going to war.

Sir R. Rodd, British Ambassador at Rome, to Sir Edward Grey.—(Received July 30.)
(Telegraphic.)   Rome, July 30, 1914.

GERMAN Ambassador told me last night that he thought Germany would be able to prevent Austria from making any exorbitant demands if Serbia could be induced to submit, and to ask for peace early, say, as soon as the occupation of Belgrade had been accomplished.

I made to his Excellency the personal suggestion that some formula might be devised by Germany which might be acceptable for an exchange of views.

I see, however, that you have already made this suggestion.

Sir Edward Grey to Sir E. Goschen, British Ambassador at Berlin.
(Telegraphic.)   Foreign Office, July 30, 1914.

YOUR telegram of 29th July.

His Majesty's Government cannot for a moment entertain the Chancellor's proposal that they should bind themselves to neutrality on such terms.

What he asks us in effect is to engage to stand by while French colonies are taken and France is beaten so long as Germany does not take French territory as distinct from the colonies.

From the material point of view such a proposal is unacceptable, for France, without further territory in Europe being taken from her, could be so crushed as to lose her position as a Great Power, and become subordinate to German policy.

Altogether apart from that, it would be a disgrace for us to make this bargain with Germany at the expense of France, a disgrace from which the good name of this country would never recover.

The Chancellor also in effect asks us to bargain away whatever obligation or interest we have as regards the neutrality of Belgium. We could not entertain that bargain either.

Having said so much it is unnecessary to examine whether the prospect of a future general neutrality agreement between England and Germany offered positive advantages sufficient to compensate us for tying our hands now. We must preserve our full freedom to act as circumstances may seem to us to require in any such unfavourable and regrettable development of the present crisis as the Chancellor contemplates.

You should speak to the Chancellor in the above sense, and add most earnestly that the one way of maintaining the good relations between England and Germany is that they should continue to work together to preserve the peace of Europe; if we succeed in this object, the mutual relations of Germany and England will, I believe, be *ipso facto* improved and strengthened. For that object His Majesty's Government will work in that way with all sincerity and good-will.

And I will say this: If the peace of Europe can be preserved, and the present crisis safely passed, my own endeavour will be to promote some arrangement to which Germany could be a party, by which she could be assured that no aggressive or hostile policy would be pursued against her or her allies by France, Russia, and ourselves, jointly or separately. I have desired this and worked for it, as far as I could, through the last Balkan crisis, and, Germany having a corresponding object, our relations sensibly improved. The idea has hitherto been too Utopian to form the subject of definite proposals, but if this present crisis, so much more acute than any that Europe has gone through for generations, be safely passed, I am hopeful that the relief and reaction which will follow may make possible some more definite rapprochement between the Powers than has been possible hitherto.

Sir Edward Grey to Sir E. Goschen, British Ambassador at Berlin.

(Telegraphic.)   Foreign Office, July 30, 1914.

I HAVE warned Prince Lichnowsky that Germany must not count upon our standing aside in all circumstances. This is doubtless the substance of the telegram from Prince Lichnowsky to German Chancellor, to which reference is made in the last two paragraphs of your telegram of 30th July.

Sir Edward Grey to Sir G. Buchanan, British Ambassador at St. Petersburgh.

(Telegraphic.)   Foreign Office, July 30, 1914.

GERMAN Ambassador informs me that German Government would endeavour to influence Austria, after taking Belgrade and Serbian territory in region of frontier, to promise not to advance further, while Powers endeavoured to arrange that Serbia should give satisfaction sufficient to pacify Austria. Territory occupied would of course be evacuated when Austria was satisfied. I suggested this yesterday as a possible relief to the situation, and, if it can be obtained, I would earnestly hope that it might be agreed to suspend further military preparations on all sides.

Russian Ambassador has told me of condition laid down by M. Sazonof, as quoted in your telegram of the 30th July, and fears it cannot be modified; but if Austrian advance were stopped after occupation of Belgrade, I think Russian Minister for Foreign Affairs' formula might be changed to read that the Powers would examine how Serbia could fully satisfy Austria without impairing Serbian sovereign rights or independence.

If Austria, having occupied Belgrade and neighbouring Serbian territory, declares herself ready, in the interest of European peace, to cease her advance and to discuss how a complete settlement can be arrived at, I hope that Russia would also consent to discussion and suspension of further military preparations, provided that other Powers did the same.

It is a slender chance of preserving peace, but the only one I can suggest if Russian Minister for Foreign Affairs can come to no agreement at Berlin. You should inform Minister for Foreign Affairs.

Sir Edward Grey to Sir F. Bertie, British Ambassador at Paris.
(Telegraphic.)   Foreign Office, July 30, 1914.

YOU should inform the Minister for Foreign Affairs of my telegram to Sir G. Buchanan of to-day, and say that I know that he has been urging Russia not to precipitate a crisis. I hope he may be able to support this last suggestion at St. Petersburgh.

Sir Edward Grey to Sir F. Bertie, British Ambassador at Paris

Sir,   Foreign Office, July 30, 1914.

M. CAMBON reminded me to-day of the letter I had written to him two years ago, in which we agreed that, if the peace of Europe was seriously threatened, we would discuss what we were prepared to do. I enclose for convenience of reference copies of the letter in question and of M. Cambon's reply. He said that the peace of Europe was never more seriously threatened than it was now. He did not wish to ask me to say directly that we would intervene, but he would like me to say what we should do if certain circumstances arose. The particular hypothesis he had in mind was an aggression by Germany on France. He gave me a paper, of which a copy is also enclosed, showing that the German military preparations were more advanced and more on the offensive upon the frontier than anything France had yet done. He antic-ipated that the aggression would take the form of either a demand that France should cease her prepa-rations, or a demand that she should engage to remain neutral if there was war between Germany and Russia. Neither of these things could France admit.

I said that the Cabinet was to meet to-morrow morning, and I would see him again to-morrow afternoon.

I am, &c.
E. GREY.

ENCLOSURE 1 .

Sir Edward Grey to M. Cambon, French Ambassador in London.

My dear Ambassador,　　　Foreign Office, November
22, 1912.

FROM time to time in recent years the French and British naval and military experts have consulted together. It has always been understood that such consultation does not restrict the freedom of either Government to decide at any future time whether or not to assist the other by armed force. We have agreed that consultation between experts is not, and ought not to be regarded as, an engagement that commits either Government to action in a contingency that has not arisen and may never arise. The disposition, for instance, of the French and British fleets respectively at the present moment is not based upon an engagement to co-operate in war.

You have, however, pointed out that, if either Government had grave reason to expect an unprovoked attack by a third Power, it might become essential to know whether it could in that event depend upon the armed assistance of the other.

I agree that, if either Government had grave reason to expect an unprovoked attack by a third Power, or something that threatened the general peace, it should immediately discuss with the other whether both Governments should act together to prevent aggression and to preserve peace, and, if so, what measures they would be prepared to take in common. If these measures involved action, the plans of the General Staffs would at once be taken into consideration, and the Governments would then decide what effect should be given to them.

Yours, &c.

E. GREY.

ENCLOSURE 2

M. Cambon, French Ambassador in London, to Sir Edward Grey.

Dear Sir Edward.   French Embassy, London.
                                   November 23, 1912.

YOU reminded me in your letter of yesterday, 22nd November, that during the last few years the military and naval authorities of France and Great Britain had consulted with each other from time to time; that it had always been understood that these consultations should not restrict the liberty of either Government to decide in the future whether they should lend each other the support of their armed forces; that, on either side, these consultations between experts were not and should not be considered as engagements binding our Governments to take action in certain eventualities; that, however, I had remarked to you that, if one or other of the two Governments had grave reasons to fear an unprovoked attack on the part of a third Power, it would become essential to know whether it could count on the armed support of the other.

Your letter answers that point, and I am authorised to state that, in the event of one of our two Governments having grave reasons to fear either an act of aggression from a third Power, or some event threatening the general peace, that Government would immediately examine with the other the question whether both Governments should act together in order to prevent the act of aggression or preserve peace. If so, the two Governments would deliberate as to the measures which they would be prepared to take in common; if those measures involved action, the two Governments would take into immediate consideration the plans of their general staffs and would then decide as to the effect to be given to those plans.

Yours &c.

PAUL CAMBON.

ENCLOSURE 3

French Minister for Foreign Affairs to M. Cambon, French Ambassador in London.
(Translation.)

THE German Army had its advance-posts on our frontiers yesterday; German patrols twice penetrated on to our territory. Our advance-posts are withdrawn to a distance of 10 kilom. from the frontier. The local population is protesting against being thus abandoned to the attack of the enemy's army, but the Government wishes to make it clear to public opinion and to the British Government that in no case will France be the aggressor. The whole 16th corps from Metz, reinforced by a part of the 8th from Trèves and Cologne, is occupying the frontier at Metz on the Luxemburg side. The 15th army corps from Strassburg has closed up on the frontier. The inhabitants of Alsace-Lorraine are prevented by the threat of being shot from crossing the frontier. Reservists have been called back to Germany by tens of thousands. This is the last stage before mobilisation, whereas we have not called back a single reservist.

As you see, Germany has done so. I would add that all my information goes to show that the German preparations began on Saturday, the very day on which the Austrian note was handed in.

These facts, added to those contained in my telegram of yesterday, will enable you to prove to the British Government the pacific intentions of the one party and the aggressive intentions of the other.

Sir R. Rodd, British Ambassador at Rome, to Sir Edward Grey.—(Received July 31.)
(Telegraphic.)   Rome, July 30, 1914.

I LEARNT from the Minister for Foreign Affairs, who sent for me this evening, that the Austrian Government had declined to continue the direct exchange of views with the Russian Government. But he had reason to believe that Germany was now disposed to give more conciliatory advice to Austria, as she seemed convinced that we should act with France and Russia, and was most anxious to avoid issue with us.

He said he was telegraphing to the Italian Ambassador at Berlin to ask the German Government to suggest that the idea of an exchange of views between the four Powers should be resumed in any form which Austria would consider acceptable. It seemed to him that Germany might invite Austria to state exactly the terms which she would demand from Serbia, and give a guarantee that she would neither deprive her of independence nor annex territory. It would be useless to ask for anything less than was contained in the Austrian ultimatum, and Germany would support no proposal that might imply non-success for Austria. We might, on the other hand, ascertain from Russia what she would accept, and, once we knew the standpoints of these two countries, discussions could be commenced at once. There was still time so long as Austria had received no check. He in any case was in favour of continuing an exchange of views with His Majesty's Government if the idea of discussions between the four Powers was impossible.

Sir E. Goschen, British Ambassador at Berlin, to Sir Edward Grey.—(Received July 31.)
(Telegraphic.)   Berlin, July 30, 1914.

I DO not know whether you have received a reply from the German Government to the communication which you made to them through the German Ambassador in London asking whether they could suggest any method by which the four Powers could use their mediating influence between Russia and Austria. I was informed last night that they had not had time to send an answer yet. To-day, in reply to an enquiry from the French Ambassador as to whether the Imperial Government had proposed any course of action, the Secretary of State said that he had felt that time would be saved by communicating with Vienna direct, and that he had asked the Austro-Hungarian Government what would satisfy them. No answer had, however, yet been returned.

The Chancellor told me last night that he was "pressing the button" as hard as he could, and that he was not sure whether he had not gone so far in urging moderation at Vienna that matters had been precipitated rather than otherwise.

FRIDAY JULY 31ST

Sir E. Goschen, British Ambassador at Berlin, to Sir Edward Grey.—(Received July 31.)
(Telegraphic.) Berlin, July 31, 1914.

CHANCELLOR informs me that his efforts to preach peace and moderation at Vienna have been seriously handicapped by the Russian mobilisation against Austria. He has done everything possible to attain his object at Vienna, perhaps even rather more than was altogether palatable at the Ballplatz. He could not, however, leave his country defenceless while time was being utilised by other Powers; and if, as he learns is the case, military measures are now being taken by Russia against Germany also, it would be impossible for him to remain quiet. He wished to tell me that it was quite possible that in a very short time, to-day perhaps, the German Government would take some very serious step; he was, in fact, just on the point of going to have an audience with the Emperor.

His Excellency added that the news of the active preparations on the Russo-German frontier had reached him just when the Czar had appealed to the Emperor, in the name of their old friendship, to mediate at Vienna, and when the Emperor was actually conforming to that request.

Sir E. Goschen, British Ambassador at Berlin, to Sir Edward Grey.—(Received July 31.)
(Telegraphic.)   Berlin, July 31, 1914.

I READ to the Chancellor this morning your answer to his appeal for British neutrality in the event of war, as contained in your telegram of yesterday. His Excellency was so taken up with the news of the Russian measures along the frontier, referred to in my immediately preceding telegram, that he received your communication without comment. He asked me to let him have the message that I had just read to him as a memorandum, as he would like to reflect upon it before giving an answer, and his mind was so full of grave matters that he could not be certain of remembering all its points. I therefore handed to him the text of your message on the understanding that it should be regarded merely as a record of conversation, and not as an official document.

His Excellency agreed.

Sir Edward Grey to Sir G. Buchanan, British Ambassador at St. Petersburgh.

(Telegraphic.)   Foreign Office, July 31, 1914.

I LEARN from the German Ambassador that, as a result of suggestions by the German Government, a conversation has taken place at Vienna between the Austrian Minister for Foreign Affairs and the Russian Ambassador. The Austrian Ambassador at St. Petersburgh has also been instructed that he may converse with the Russian Minister for Foreign Affairs, and that he should give explanations about the Austrian ultimatum to Serbia, and discuss suggestions and any questions directly affecting Austro-Russian relations. If the Russian Government object to the Austrians mobilising eight army corps, it might be pointed out that this is not too great a number against 400,000 Serbians.

The German Ambassador asked me to urge the Russian Government to show goodwill in the discussions and to suspend their military preparations.

It is with great satisfaction that I have learnt that discussions are being resumed between Austria and Russia, and you should express this to the Minister for Foreign Affairs and tell him that I earnestly hope he will encourage them.

I informed the German Ambassador that, as

regards military preparations, I did not see how Russia could be urged to suspend them unless some limit were put by Austria to the advance of her troops into Serbia.

Sir. Edward Grey to Sir E. Goschen, British Ambassador at Berlin.
(Telegraphic.)   Foreign Office, July 31, 1913.

I HOPE that the conversations which are now proceeding between Austria and Russia may lead to a satisfactory result. The stumbling-block hitherto has been Austrian mistrust of Serbian assurances, and Russian mistrust of Austrian intentions with regard to the independence and integrity of Serbia. It has occurred to me that, in the event of this mistrust preventing a solution being found by Vienna and St. Petersburgh, Germany might sound Vienna, and I would undertake to sound St. Petersburgh, whether it would be possible for the four disinterested Powers to offer to Austria that they would undertake to see that she obtained full satisfaction of her demands on Serbia, provided that they did not impair Serbian sovereignty and the integrity of Serbian territory. As your Excellency is aware, Austria has already declared her willingness to respect them. Russia might be informed by the four Powers that they would undertake to prevent Austrian demands going the length of impairing Serbian sovereignty and integrity. All Powers would of course suspend further military operations or preparations.

You may sound the Secretary of State about this proposal.

I said to German Ambassador this morning that if Germany could get any reasonable proposal put forward which made it clear that Germany and Austria were striving to preserve European peace, and that Russia and France would be unreasonable if they rejected it, I would support it at St. Petersburgh and Paris, and go the length of saying that if Russia and France would not accept it His Majesty's Government would have nothing more to do with the consequences; but, otherwise, I told German Ambassador that if France became involved we should be drawn in.

You can add this when sounding Chancellor or Secretary of State as to proposal above.

Sir E. Goschen, British Ambassador at Berlin, to Sir Edward Grey.—(Received July 31.)

(Telegraphic.)   Berlin, July 31, 1914.

ACCORDING to information just received by German Government from their Ambassador at St. Petersburgh, whole Russian army and fleet are being mobilised. Chancellor tells me that "Kriegsgefahr" will be proclaimed at once by German Government, as it can only be against Germany that Russian general mobilisation is directed. Mobilisation would follow almost immediately. His Excellency added in explanation that "Kriegsgefahr" signified the taking of certain precautionary measures consequent upon strained relations with a foreign country.

This news from St. Petersburgh, added his Excellency, seemed to him to put an end to all hope of a peaceful solution of the crisis. Germany must certainly prepare for all emergencies.

I asked him whether he could not still put pressure on the authorities at Vienna to do something in general interests to reassure Russia and to show themselves disposed to continue discussions on a friendly basis. He replied that last night he had begged Austria to reply to your last proposal, and that he had received a reply to the effect that Austrian Minister for Foreign Affairs would take wishes of the Emperor this morning in the matter.

Sir G. Buchanan, British Ambassador at St. Petersburgh, to Sir Edward Grey.—(Received July 31.)
(Telegraphic.)   St. Petersburgh, July 31, 1914.

IT has been decided to issue orders for general mobilisation.

This decision was taken in consequence of report received from Russian Ambassador in Vienna to the effect that Austria is determined not to yield to intervention of Powers, and that she is moving troops against Russia as well as against Serbia.

Russia has also reason to believe that Germany is making active military preparations, and she cannot afford to let her get a start.

Sir Edward Grey to Sir F. Bertie, British Ambassador at Paris, and Sir E. Goschen, British Ambassador at Berlin.
(Telegraphic.)   Foreign Office, July 31, 1914.

I STILL trust that situation is not irretrievable, but in view of prospect of mobilisation in Germany it becomes essential to His Majesty's Government, in view of existing treaties, to ask whether French (German) Government are prepared to engage to respect neutrality of Belgium so long as no other Power violates it.

A similar request is being addressed to German (French) Government. It is important to have an early answer.

Sir Edward Grey to Sir F. Villiers, British Minister at Brussels.
(Telegraphic.)   Foreign Office, July 31, 1914.

IN view of existing treaties, you should inform Minister for Foreign Affairs that, in consideration of the possibility of a European war, I have asked French and German Governments whether each is prepared to respect the neutrality of Belgium provided it is violated by no other Power.

You should say that I assume that the Belgian Government will maintain to the utmost of their power their neutrality, which I desire and expect other Power to uphold and observe.

You should inform the Belgian Government that an early reply is desired.

Sir Edward Grey to Sir F. Bertie, British Ambassador at Paris.
(Telegraphic.)   Foreign Office, July 31, 1914.

I HAVE received your telegram of yesterday's date.

Nobody here feels that in this dispute, so far as it has yet gone, British treaties or obligations are involved. Feeling is quite different from what it was during the Morocco question. That crisis involved a dispute directly involving France, whereas in this case France is being drawn into a dispute which is not hers.

I believe it to be quite untrue that our attitude has been a decisive factor in situation. German Government do not expect our neutrality.

We cannot undertake a definite pledge to intervene in a war. I have so told the French Ambassador, who has urged His Majesty's Government to reconsider this decision.

I have told him that we should not be justified in giving any pledge at the present moment, but that we will certainly consider the situation again directly there is a new development.

Sir F. Bertie, British Ambassador at Paris, to Sir Edward Grey.—(Received July 31.)
(Telegraphic.)   Paris, July 31, 1914.

AT 7 o'clock this evening I was sent for by Minister for Foreign Affairs. When I arrived the German Ambassador was leaving his Excellency.

German Ambassador had informed his Excellency that, in view of the fact that orders had been given for the total mobilisation of Russian army and fleet, German Government have in an ultimatum which they have addressed to the Russian Government required that Russian forces should be demobilised.

The German Government will consider it necessary to order the total mobilisation of the German army on the Russian and French frontiers if within twelve hours the Russian Government do not give an undertaking to comply with German demand.

The Minister for Foreign Affairs asks me to communicate this to you, and enquires what, in these circumstances, will be the attitude of England.

German Ambassador could not say when the twelve hours terminates. He is going to call at the Ministry for Foreign Affairs to-morrow (Saturday) at 1 P.M. in order to receive the French Government's answer as to the attitude they will adopt in the circumstances.

He intimated the possibility of his requiring his passports.

I am informed by the Russian Ambassador that he is not aware of any general mobilisation of the Russian forces having taken place.

Sir M. de Bunsen, British Ambassador at Vienna, to Sir Edward Grey.—(Received July 31.)
(Telegraphic.)   Vienna, July 31, 1914.

I AM informed by Count Forgach, Under-Secretary of State, that although Austria was compelled to respond to Russian mobilisation, which he deplored, the Austrian Ambassador in London has received instructions to inform you that mobilisation was not to be regarded as a necessarily hostile act on either side. Telegrams were being exchanged between the Emperor of Russia and the German Emperor, and conversations were proceeding between Austrian Ambassador at St. Petersburgh and Russian Minister for Foreign Affairs. A general war might, he seriously hoped, be staved off by these efforts. On my expressing my fear that Germany would mobilise, he said that Germany must do something, in his opinion, to secure her position. As regards Russian intervention on behalf of Serbia, Austria-Hungary found it difficult to recognise such a claim. I called his attention to the fact that during the discussion of the Albanian frontier at the London Conference of Ambassadors the Russian Government had stood behind Serbia, and that a compromise between the views of Russia and Austria-Hungary resulted with accepted frontier line. Although he spoke in a conciliatory tone, and did not regard the situation as desperate, I could not get from him any suggestion for a similar compromise in the present case. Count Forgach is going this afternoon to see the Russian Ambassador, whom I have informed of the above conversation.

The Russian Ambassador has explained that Russia has no desire to interfere unduly with Serbia; that, as compared with the late Russian Minister, the present Minister at Belgrade is a man of very moderate views; and that, as regards Austrian demands, Russia had counselled Serbia to yield to them as far as she possibly could without sacrificing her independence. His Excellency is exerting himself strongly in the interests of peace.

Sir Edward Grey to Sir F. Bertie, British Ambassador at Paris.

Sir,   Foreign Office, July 31, 1914.

M. CAMBON referred to-day to a telegram that had been shown to Sir Arthur Nicolson this morning from the French Ambassador in Berlin, saying that it was the uncertainty with regard to whether we would intervene which was the encouraging element in Berlin, and that, if we would only declare definitely on the side of Russia and France, it would decide the German attitude in favour of peace.

I said that it was quite wrong to suppose that we had left Germany under the impression that we would not intervene. I had refused overtures to promise that we should remain neutral. I had not only definitely declined to say that we would remain neutral, I had even gone so far this morning as to say to the German Ambassador that, if France and Germany became involved in war, we should be drawn into it. That, of course, was not the same thing as taking an engagement to France, and I told M. Cambon of it only to show that we had not left Germany under the impression that we would stand aside.

M. Cambon then asked me for my reply to what he had said yesterday.

I said that we had come to the conclusion, in the Cabinet to-day, that we could not give any pledge at the present time. Though we should have to put our policy before Parliament, we could not pledge Parliament in advance. Up to the present moment, we did not feel, and public opinion did not feel, that any treaties or obligations of this country were involved. Further developments might alter this situation and cause the Government and Parliament to take the view that intervention was justified. The preservation of the neutrality of Belgium might be, I would not say a decisive, but an important factor, in determining our attitude. Whether we proposed to Parliament to intervene or not to intervene in a war, Parliament would wish to know how we stood with regard to the neutrality of Belgium, and it might be that I should ask both France and Germany whether each was prepared to undertake an engagement that she would not be the first to violate the neutrality of Belgium.

M. Cambon repeated his question whether we would help France if Germany made an attack on her.

I said that I could only adhere to the answer that, as far as things had gone at present, we could not take any engagement.

M. Cambon urged that Germany had from the beginning rejected proposals that might have made for peace. It could not be to England's interest that France should be crushed by Germany. We should then be in a very diminished position with regard to Germany. In 1870 we had made a great mistake in allowing an enormous increase of German strength, and we should now be repeating the mistake. He asked me whether I could not submit his question to the Cabinet again.

I said that the Cabinet would certainly be summoned as soon as there was some new development, but at the present moment the only answer I could give was that we could not undertake any definite engagement.

I am, &c.

E. GREY.

Sir G. Buchanan, British Ambassador at St. Petersburgh, to Sir Edward Grey.—(Received August 1.)
(Telegraphic.)   St. Petersburgh, July 31, 1914.

MINISTER for Foreign Affairs sent for me and French Ambassador and asked us to telegraph to our respective Governments subjoined formula as best calculated to amalgamate proposal made by you in your telegram of 30th July with formula recorded in my telegram of 30th July. He trusted it would meet with your approval:—

"If Austria will agree to check the advance of her troops on Serbian territory; if, recognising that the dispute between Austria and Serbia has assumed a character of European interest, she will allow the Great Powers to look into the matter and determine whether Serbia could satisfy the Austro-Hungarian Government without impairing her rights as a sovereign State or her independence, Russia will undertake to maintain her waiting attitude."

His Excellency then alluded to the telegram sent to German Emperor by Emperor of Russia in reply to the former's telegram. He said that Emperor Nicholas had begun by thanking Emperor William for his telegram and for the hopes of peaceful solution which it held out. His Majesty had then proceeded to assure Emperor William that no intention whatever of an aggressive character was concealed behind Russian military preparations. So long as conversation with Austria continued, His Imperial Majesty undertook that not a single man should be moved across the frontier; it was, however of course impossible, for reasons explained, to stop a mobilisation which was already in progress.

M. Sazonof said that undoubtedly there would be better prospect of a peaceful solution if the suggested conversation were to take place in London, where the atmosphere was far more favourable, and he therefore hoped that you would see your way to agreeing to this.

His Excellency ended by expressing his deep gratitude to His Majesty's Government, who had done so much to save the situation. It would be largely due to them if war were prevented. The Emperor, the Russian Government, and the Russian people would never forget the firm attitude adopted by Great Britain.

Sir E. Goschen, British Ambassador at Berlin, to Sir Edward Grey.—(Received August 1.)
(Telegraphic.)   Berlin, July 31, 1914.

YOUR telegram of 31st July.

I spent an hour with Secretary of State urging him most earnestly to accept your proposal and make another effort to prevent terrible catastrophe of a European war.

He expressed himself very sympathetically towards your proposal, and appreciated your continued efforts to maintain peace, but said it was impossible for the Imperial Government to consider any proposal until they had received an answer from Russia to their communication of to-day; this communication, which he admitted had the form of an ultimatum, being that, unless Russia could inform the Imperial Government within twelve hours that she would immediately countermand her mobilisation against Germany and Austria, Germany would be obliged on her side to mobilise at once.

I asked his Excellency why they had made their demand even more difficult for Russia to accept by asking them to demobilise in south as well. He replied that it was in order to prevent Russia from saying all her mobilisation was only directed against Austria.

His Excellency said that if the answer from Russia was satisfactory he thought personally that your proposal merited favourable consideration, and in any case he would lay it before the Emperor and Chancellor, but he repeated that it was no use discussing it until the Russian Government had sent in their answer to the German demand.

He again assured me that both the Emperor William, at the request of the Emperor of Russia, and the German Foreign Office had even up till last night been urging Austria to show willingness to continue discussions—and telegraphic and telephonic communications from Vienna had been of a promising nature—but Russia's mobilisation had spoilt everything.

Sir E. Goschen, British Ambassador at Berlin, to Sir Edward Grey.—(Received August 1.)
(Telegraphic.)   Berlin, July 31, 1914.

NEUTRALITY of Belgium, referred to in your telegram of 31st July to Sir F. Bertie.

I have seen Secretary of State, who informs me that he must consult the Emperor and the Chancellor before he could possibly answer. I gathered from what he said that he thought any reply they might give could not but disclose a certain amount of their plan of campaign in the event of war ensuing, and he was therefore very doubtful whether they would return any answer at all. His Excellency, nevertheless, took note of your request.

It appears from what he said that German Government consider that certain hostile acts have already been committed by Belgium. As an instance of this, he alleged that a consignment of corn for Germany had been placed under an embargo already.

I hope to see his Excellency to-morrow again to discuss the matter further, but the prospect of obtaining a definite answer seems to me remote.

In speaking to me to-day the Chancellor made it

clear that Germany would in any case desire to know the reply returned to you by the French Government.

Sir Edward Grey to Sir E. Goschen, British Ambassador at Berlin.

Sir,   Foreign Office, August 1, 1914.

I TOLD the German Ambassador to-day that the reply of the German Government with regard to the neutrality of Belgium was a matter of very great regret, because the neutrality of Belgium affected feeling in this country. If Germany could see her way to give the same assurance as that which had been given by France it would materially contribute to relieve anxiety and tension here. On the other hand, if there were a violation of the neutrality of Belgium by one combatant while the other respected it, it would be extremely difficult to restrain public feeling in this country. I said that we had been discussing this question at a Cabinet meeting, and as I was autho-rised to tell him this I gave him a memorandum of it.

He asked me whether, if Germany gave a promise not to violate Belgium neutrality we would engage to remain neutral.

I replied that I could not say that; our hands were still free, and we were considering what our attitude should be. All I could say was that our attitude would be determined largely by public opinion here, and that the neutrality of Belgium would appeal very strongly to public opinion here. I did not think that we could give a promise of neutrality on that condi-tion alone.

The Ambassador pressed me as to whether I could not formulate conditions on which we would remain neutral. He even suggested that the integrity of France and her colonies might be guaranteed.

I said that I felt obliged to refuse definitely any promise to remain neutral on similar terms, and I could only say that we must keep our hands free.

I am, &c.

E. GREY.

Sir F. Bertie, British Ambassador at Paris, to Sir Edward Grey.—(Received August 1.)

(Telegraphic.) Paris, July 31, 1914.

ON the receipt at 8.30 to-night of your telegram of this afternoon, I sent a message to Minister for Foreign Affairs requesting to see him. He received me at 10.30 to-night at the Elysée, where a Cabinet Council was being held. He took a note of the enquiry as to the respecting by France of the neutrality of Belgium which you instructed me to make.

He told me that a communication had been made to you by the German Ambassador in London of the intention of Germany to order a general mobilisation of her army if Russia do not demobilise at once. He is urgently anxious as to what the attitude of England will be in the circumstances, and begs an answer may be made by His Majesty's Government at the earliest moment possible.

Minister for Foreign Affairs also told me that the German Embassy is packing up.

Sir F. Bertie, British Ambassador at Paris, to Sir Edward Grey.—(Received August 1.)
(Telegraphic.)   Paris, July 31, 1914.

MY immediately preceding telegram.

Political Director has brought me the reply of the Minister for Foreign Affairs to your enquiry respecting the neutrality of Belgium. It is as follows:—

French Government are resolved to respect the neutrality of Belgium, and it would only be in the event of some other Power violating that neutrality that France might find herself under the necessity, in order to assure defence of her own security, to act otherwise. This assurance has been given several times. President of the Republic spoke of it to the King of the Belgians, and the French Minister at Brussels has spontaneously renewed the assurance to the Belgian Minister for Foreign Affairs to-day.

SATURDAY AUGUST 1ST

Sir F. Bertie, British Ambassador at Paris, to Sir Edward Grey.—(Received August 1.)
(Telegraphic.)   Paris, August 1, 1914.

I HAVE had conversation with the Political Director, who states that the German Ambassador was informed, on calling at the Ministry for Foreign Affairs this morning, that the French Government failed to comprehend the reason which prompted his communication of yesterday evening. It was pointed out to his Excellency that general mobilisation in Russia had not been ordered until after Austria had decreed a general mobilisation, and that the Russian Government were ready to demobilise if all Powers did likewise. It seemed strange to the French Government that in view of this and of the fact that Russia and Austria were ready to converse, the German Government should have at that moment presented an ultimatum at St. Petersburgh requiring immediate demobilisation by Russia. There were no differences at issue between France and Germany, but the German Ambassador had made a menacing communication to the French Government and had requested an answer the next day, intimating that he would have to break off relations and leave Paris if the reply were not satisfactory. The Ambassador was informed that the French Government considered that this was an extraordinary proceeding.

The German Ambassador, who is to see the Minister for Foreign Affairs again this evening, said nothing about demanding his passports, but he stated that he had packed up.

Sir M. de Bunsen, British Ambassador at Vienna, to Sir Edward Grey.—(Received August 1.)
(Telegraphic.)   Vienna, August 1, 1914.

GENERAL mobilisation of army and fleet.

Sir F. Villiers, British Minister at Brussels, to Sir Edward Grey.—(Received August 1.)
(Telegraphic.)   Brussels, August 1, 1914.

BELGIAN neutrality.

The instructions conveyed in your telegram of yesterday have been acted upon.

Belgium expects and desires that other Powers will observe and uphold her neutrality, which she intends to maintain to the utmost of her power. In so informing me, Minister for Foreign Affairs said that, in the event of the violation of the neutrality of their territory, they believed that they were in a position to defend themselves against intrusion. The relations between Belgium and her neighbours were excellent, and there was no reason to suspect their intentions; but he thought it well, nevertheless, to be prepared against emergencies.

Minister of State, Luxemburg, to Sir Edward Grey.— *(Received August 2.)*
(Translation.)
(Telegraphic.) Luxemburg, August 2, 1914.

The Luxemburg Minister of State, Eyshen, has just received through the German Minister in Luxemburg, M. de Buch, a telegram from the Chancellor of the German Empire, Bethmann-Hollweg, to the effect that the military measures taken in Luxemburg do not constitute a hostile act against Luxemburg, but are only intended to insure against a possible attack of a French army. Full compensation will be paid to Luxemburg for any damage caused by using the railways which are leased to the Empire.

Sir Edward Grey to Sir E. Goschen, British Ambassador at Berlin.

(Telegraphic.)   Foreign Office, August 1, 1914.

WE are informed that authorities at Hamburg have forcibly detained steamers belonging to the Great Central Company and other British merchant-ships.

I cannot ascertain on what grounds the detention of British ships has been ordered.

You should request German Government to send immediate orders that they should be allowed to proceed without delay. The effect on public opinion here will be deplorable unless this is done. His Majesty's Government, on their side, are most anxious to avoid any incident of an aggressive nature, and the German Government will, I hope, be equally careful not to take any step which would make the situation between us impossible.

Sir Edward Grey to Sir E. Goschen, British Ambassador at Berlin.

(Telegraphic.)   Foreign Office, August 1, 1914.

I STILL believe that it might be possible to secure peace if only a little respite in time can be gained before any Great Power begins war.

The Russian Government has communicated to me the readiness of Austria to discuss with Russia and the readiness of Austria to accept a basis of mediation which is not open to the objections raised in regard to the formula which Russia originally suggested.

Things ought not to be hopeless so long as Austria and Russia are ready to converse, and I hope that German Government may be able to make use of the Russian communications referred to above, in order to avoid tension. His Majesty's Government are carefully abstaining from any act which may precipitate matters.

Sir Edward Grey to Sir E. Goschen, British Ambassador at Berlin.
(Telegraphic.)   Foreign Office, August 1, 1914.

FOLLOWING telegram from M. Sazonof to Count Benckendorff (Urgent.)

"Formula amended in accordance with the English proposal: 'If Austria consents to stay the march of her troops on Serbian territory, and if, recognising that the Austro-Serbian conflict has assumed the character of a question of European interest, she admits that the Great Powers may examine the satisfaction which Serbia can accord to the Austro-Hungarian Government without injury to her sovereign rights as a State and to her independence, Russia undertakes to preserve her waiting attitude.'"

(Above communicated to all the Powers.)

Sir Edward Grey to Sir E. Goschen, British Ambassador at Berlin.
(Telegraphic.)   Foreign Office, August 1, 1914.

M. DE ETTER came to-day to communicate the contents of a telegram from M. Sazonof, dated the 31st July, which are as follows:—

"The Austro-Hungarian Ambassador declared the readiness of his Government to discuss the substance of the Austrian ultimatum to Serbia. M. Sazonof replied by expressing his satisfaction, and said it was desirable that the discussions should take place in London with the participation of the Great Powers.

"M. Sazonof hoped that the British Government would assume the direction of these discussions. The whole of Europe would be thankful to them. It would be very important that Austria should meanwhile put a stop provisionally to her military action on Serbian territory."

(The above has been communicated to the six Powers.)

Sir F. Bertie, British Ambassador at Paris, to Sir Edward Grey.—(Received August 1.)

(Telegraphic.)   Paris, August 1, 1914.

PRESIDENT of the Republic has informed me that German Government were trying to saddle Russia with the responsibility; that it was only after a decree of general mobilisation had been issued in Austria that the Emperor of Russia ordered a general mobilisation; that, although the measures which the German Government have already taken are in effect a general mobilisation, they are not so designated; that a French general mobilisation will become necessary in self-defence, and that France is already forty-eight hours behind Germany as regards German military preparations; that the French troops have orders not to go nearer to the German frontier than a distance of 10 kilom. so as to avoid any grounds for accusations of provocation to Germany, whereas the German troops, on the other hand, are actually on the French frontier and have made incursions on it; that, notwithstanding mobilisations, the Emperor of Russia has expressed himself ready to continue his conversations with the German Ambassador with a view to preserving the peace; that French Government, whose wishes are markedly pacific, sincerely desire the preservation of peace and do not quite despair, even now, of its being possible to avoid war.

Sir Edward Grey to Sir G. Buchanan, British Ambassador at St. Petersburgh.
(Telegraphic.)   Foreign Office, August 1, 1914.

INFORMATION reaches me from a most reliable source that Austrian Government have informed German Government that though the situation has been changed by the mobilisation of Russia they would in full appreciation of the efforts of England for the preservation of peace be ready to consider favourably my proposal for mediation between Austria and Serbia. The effect of this acceptance would naturally be that the Austrian military action against Serbia would continue for the present, and that the British Government would urge upon

Russian Government to stop the mobilisation of troops directed against Austria, in which case Austria would naturally cancel those defensive military counter-measures in Galicia, which have been forced upon Austria by Russian mobilisation.

You should inform Minister for Foreign Affairs and say that if, in the consideration of the acceptance of mediation by Austria, Russia can agree to stop mobilisation, it appears still to be possible to preserve peace. Presumably the matter should be discussed with German Government also by Russian Government.

Sir F. Bertie, British Ambassador at Paris, to Sir Edward Grey.—(Received August 1.)

(Telegraphic.)   Paris, August 1, 1914.

MINISTER of War informed military attaché this afternoon that orders had been given at 3.40 for a general mobilisation of the French Army. This became necessary because the Minister of War knows that, under the system of "Kriegszustand," the Germans have called up six classes. Three classes are sufficient to bring their covering troops up to war strength, the remaining three being the reserve. This, he says, being tantamount to mobilisation, is mobilisation under another name.

The French forces on the frontier have opposed to them eight army corps on a war footing, and an attack is expected at any moment. It is therefore of the utmost importance to guard against this. A zone of 10 kilom. has been left between the French troops and German frontier. The French troops will not attack, and the Minister of War is anxious that it should be explained that this act of mobilisation is one for purely defensive purposes.

Sir Edward Grey to Sir M. de Bunsen, British Ambassador at Vienna.
(Telegraphic.)   Foreign Office, August 1, 1914.

I SAW the Austro-Hungarian Ambassador this morning. He supplied me with the substance of a telegram which the Austro-Hungarian Minister for Foreign Affairs had sent to the Austrian Ambassador in Paris. In this telegram his Excellency was given instructions to assure the French Minister for Foreign Affairs that there was no intention in the minds of the Austro-Hungarian Government to impair the sovereign rights of Serbia or to obtain territorial aggrandisement. The Ambassador added that he was further instructed to inform the French Minister for Foreign Affairs that there was no truth in the report which had been published in Paris to the effect that Austria-Hungary intended to occupy the sanjak.

Count Mensdorff called again later at the Foreign Office. He informed me of a telegram sent yesterday to the Austro-Hungarian Ambassador at St. Petersburgh by Count Berchtold, and gave me the substance.

It states that Count Berchtold begged the Russian Ambassador, whom he sent for yesterday, to do his best to remove the wholly erroneous impression in St. Petersburgh that the "door had been banged" by Austria-Hungary on all further conversations. The Russian Ambassador promised to do this. Count Berchtold repeated on this occasion to the Russian Ambassador the assurance which had already been given at St. Petersburgh, to the effect that neither an infraction of Serbian sovereign rights nor the acquisition of Serbian territory was being contemplated by Austria-Hungary.

Special attention was called by Count Mensdorff to the fact that this telegram contains a statement to the effect that conversations at St. Petersburgh had not been broken off by Austria-Hungary.

Sir E. Goschen, British Ambassador at Berlin, to Sir Edward Grey.—(Received August 2.)
(Telegraphic.)   Berlin, August 1, 1914.

YOUR telegram of to-day.

I have communicated the substance of the above telegram to the Secretary of State, and spent a long time arguing with him that the chief dispute was between Austria and Russia, and that Germany was only drawn in as Austria's ally. If therefore Austria and Russia were, as was evident, ready to discuss matters and Germany did not desire war on her own account, it seemed to me only logical that Germany should hold her hand and continue to work for a peaceful settlement. Secretary of State said that Austria's readiness to discuss was the result of German influence at

Vienna, and, had not Russia mobilised against Germany, all would have been well. But Russia by abstaining from answering Germany's demand that she should demobilise, had caused Germany to mobilise also. Russia had said that her mobilisation did not necessarily imply war, and that she could perfectly well remain mobilised for months without making war. This was not the case with Germany. She had the speed and Russia had the numbers, and the safety of the German Empire forbade that Germany should allow Russia time to bring up masses of troops from all parts of her wide dominions. The situation now was that, though the Imperial Government had allowed her several hours beyond the specified time, Russia had sent no answer. Germany had therefore ordered mobilisation, and the German representative at St. Petersburgh had been instructed within a certain time to inform the Russian Government that the Imperial Government must regard their refusal to an answer as creating a state of war.

Sir G. Buchanan, British Ambassador at St. Petersburgh, to Sir Edward Grey.—(Received August 2.)
(Telegraphic.)   St. Petersburgh, August 1, 1914.

MY telegram of 31st July.

The Emperor of Russia read his telegram to the German Emperor to the German Ambassador at the audience given to his Excellency yesterday. No progress whatever was made.

In the evening M. Sazonof had an interview

with the Austrian Ambassador who, not being definitely instructed by his Government, did his best to
deflect the conversation towards a general discussion
of the relations between Austria-Hungary and Russia
instead of keeping to the question of Serbia. In reply
the Minister for Foreign Affairs expressed his desire
that these relations should remain friendly, and said
that, taken in general, they were perfectly satisfactory;
but the real question which they had to solve at this
moment was whether Austria was to crush Serbia and
to reduce her to the status of a vassal, or whether she
was to leave Serbia a free and independent State. In
these circumstances, while the Serbian question was
unsolved, the abstract discussion of the relations
between Austria-Hungary and Russia was a waste of
time. The only place where a successful discussion of
this question could be expected was London, and any
such discussion was being made impossible by the
action of Austria-Hungary in subjecting Belgrade, a
virtually unfortified town, to bombardment.

M. Sazonof informed the French Ambassador
and myself this morning of his conversation with the
Austrian Ambassador. He went on to say that during
the Balkan crisis he had made it clear to the Austrian
Government that war with Russia must inevitably
follow an Austrian attack on Serbia. It was clear that
Austrian domination of Serbia was as intolerable for
Russia as the dependence of the Netherlands on
Germany would be to Great Britain. It was in fact,
for Russia a question of life and death. The policy of
Austria had throughout been both tortuous and

immoral, and she thought that she could treat Russia
with defiance, secure in the support of her German
ally. Similarly the policy of Germany had been an
equivocal and double-faced policy, and it mattered
little whether the German Government knew or did
not know the terms of the Austrian ultimatum; what
mattered was that her intervention with the Austrian
Government had been postponed until the moment
had passed when its influence would have been felt.
Germany was unfortunate in her representatives in
Vienna and St. Petersburgh: the former was a violent
Russophobe who had urged Austria on, the latter
had reported to his Government that Russia would
never go to war. M. Sazonof was completely weary
of the ceaseless endeavours he had made to avoid a
war. No suggestion held out to him had been
refused. He had accepted the proposal for a conference of four, for mediation by Great Britain and
Italy, for direct conversation between Austria and
Russia; but Germany and Austria-Hungary had
either rendered these attempts for peace ineffective
by evasive replies or had refused them altogether.
The action of the Austro-Hungarian Government
and the German preparations had forced the Russian
Government to order mobilisation, and the mobilisation of Germany had created a desperate situation.

M. Sazonof added that the formula, of which the
text is contained in my telegram of 31st July, had
been forwarded by the Russian Government to
Vienna, and he would adhere to it if you could
obtain its acceptance before the frontier was crossed

by German troops. In no case would Russia begin hostilities first.

I now see no possibility of a general war being avoided unless the agreement of France and Germany can be obtained to keep their armies mobilised on their own sides of the frontier, as Russia has expressed her readiness to do, pending a last attempt to reach a settlement of the present crisis.

Sir F. Bertie, British Ambassador at Paris, to Sir Edward Grey.—(Received August 1.)
(Telegraphic.)   Paris, August 1, 1914.

THE Minister of War again sent for the military attaché this evening, as he said he wished to keep him informed of the situation. He laid great stress on the fact that the zone of 10 kilom., which he had arranged between the French troops and the German frontier, and which was still occupied by peasants, was a proof of the French endeavours to commit no provocative act.

Sir M. de Bunsen, British Ambassador at Vienna, to Sir Edward Grey.—(Received August 2.)
(Telegraphic.)   Vienna, August 1, 1914.

I AM to be received to-morrow by Minister for Foreign Affairs. This afternoon he is to see the French and Russian Ambassadors. I have just been informed by the Russian Ambassador of German ultimatum requiring that Russia should demobilise within twelve hours. On being asked by the Russian Minister for Foreign Affairs whether the inevitable refusal of Russia to yield to this curt summons meant war, the German Ambassador replied that Germany would be forced to mobilise if Russia refused. Russian Ambassador at Vienna thinks that war is almost inevitable, and that as mobilisation is too expensive to be kept for long, Germany will attack Russia at once. He says that the so-called mobilisation of Russia amounted to nothing more than that Russia had taken military measures corresponding to those taken by Germany. There seems to be even greater tension between Germany and Russia than there is between Austria and Russia. Russia would, according to the Russian Ambassador, be satisfied even now with assurance respecting Serbian integrity and independence. He says that Russia had no intention to attack Austria. He is going again to-day to point out to the Minister for Foreign Affairs that most terrific consequences must ensue from refusal to make this slight concession. This time Russia would fight to the last extremity. I agree with his Excellency that the German Ambassador at Vienna desired war from the first, and that his strong personal bias probably coloured his action here. The Russian Ambassador is convinced that the German Government also desired war from the first.

It is the intention of the French Ambassador to speak earnestly to the Minister for Foreign Affairs to-day on the extreme danger of the situation, and to ask whether proposals to serve as a basis of mediation from any quarter are being considered. There is great anxiety to know what England will do. I fear that nothing can alter the determination of Austro-Hungarian Government to proceed on their present course, if they have made up their mind with the approval of Germany.

Sir E. Goschen, British Ambassador at Berlin, to Sir Edward Grey.—(Received August 2.)
(Telegraphic.)   Berlin, August 1, 1914.

ORDERS have just been issued for the general mobilisation of the navy and army, the first day of mobilisation to be 2nd August.

Sir E. Goschen, British Ambassador at Berlin, to Sir Edward Grey.—(Received August 2.)
(Telegraphic.)   Berlin, August 1, 1914.

DETENTION of British merchant ships at Hamburg.

Your telegram of 1st August acted on.

Secretary of State, who expressed the greatest surprise and annoyance, has promised to send orders at once to allow steamers to proceed without delay.

SUNDAY AUGUST 2ND
– TUESDAY AUGUST 4TH

Sir E. Goschen, British Ambassador at Berlin, to Sir Edward Grey.—(Received August 2.)

(Telegraphic.)   Berlin, August 2, 1914.

SECRETARY of State has just informed me that, owing to certain Russian troops having crossed frontier, Germany and Russia are now in a state of war.

Sir E. Goschen, British Ambassador at Berlin, to Sir Edward Grey.—(Received August 2.)

(Telegraphic.)   Berlin, August 2, 1914.

MY telegram of 1st August.

Secretary of State informs me that orders were sent last night to allow British ships in Hamburg to proceed on their way. He says that this must be regarded as a special favour to His Majesty's Government, as no other foreign ships have been allowed to leave. Reason of detention was that mines were being laid and other precautions being taken.

Sir F. Villiers, British Minister at Brussels, to Sir Edward Grey.—(Received August 2.)
(Telegraphic.)   Brussels, August 2, 1914.

THE news that a German force has entered Grand Duchy of Luxemburg has been officially confirmed to the Belgian Government.

Minister of State, Luxemburg, to Sir Edward Grey.—(Received August 2.)
(Translation.)   *Luxemburg,*
(Telegraphic.)   August 2, 1914.

I HAVE the honour to bring to your Excellency's notice the following facts:—

On Sunday, the 2nd August, very early, the German troops, according to the information which has up to now reached the Grand Ducal Government, penetrated into Luxemburg territory by the bridges of Wasserbillig and Remich, and proceeded particularly towards the south and in the direction of Luxemburg, the capital of the Grand

Duchy. A certain number of armoured trains with troops and ammunition have been sent along the railway line from Wasserbillig to Luxemburg, where their arrival is expected. These occurrences constitute acts which are manifestly contrary to the neutrality of the Grand Duchy as guaranteed by the Treaty of London of 1867. The Luxemburg Government have not failed to address an energetic protest against this aggression to the representatives of His Majesty the German Emperor at Luxemburg. An identical protest will be sent by telegraph to the Secretary of State for Foreign Affairs at Berlin.

Sir Edward Grey to Sir F. Bertie, British Ambassador at Paris.

(Telegraphic.) Foreign Office, August 2, 1914.

AFTER the Cabinet this morning I gave M. Cambon the following memorandum:—

"I am authorised to give an assurance that, if the German fleet comes into the Channel or through the North Sea to undertake hostile operations against French coasts or shipping, the British fleet will give all the protection in its power.

"This assurance is of course subject to the policy of His Majesty's Government receiving the support of Parliament, and must not be taken as binding His Majesty's Government to take any action until the above contingency of action by the German fleet takes place."

I pointed out that we had very large questions and most difficult issues to consider, and that Government felt that they could not bind themselves to declare war upon Germany necessarily if war broke out between France and Germany to-morrow, but it was essential to the French Government, whose fleet had long been concentrated in the Mediterranean, to know how to make their dispositions with their north coast entirely undefended. We therefore thought it necessary to give them this assurance. It did not bind us to go to war with Germany unless the German fleet took the action indicated, but it did give a security to France that would enable her to settle the disposition of her own Mediterranean fleet.

M. Cambon asked me about the violation of Luxemburg. I told him the doctrine on that point laid down by Lord Derby and Lord Clarendon in 1867. He asked me what we should say about the violation of the neutrality of Belgium. I said that was a much more important matter; we were considering what state-ment we should make in Parliament to-morrow—in effect, whether we should declare violation of Belgian neutrality to be a *casus belli*. I told him what had been said to the German Ambassador on this point.

Sir Edward Grey to Sir E. Goschen, British Ambassador at Berlin.
(Telegraphic.)   Foreign Office, August 2, 1914.

YOUR telegram of 1st August.

I regret to learn that 100 tons of sugar was com-pulsorily unloaded from the British steamship "Sappho" at Hamburg and detained. Similar action appears to have been taken with regard to other British vessels loaded with sugar.

You should inform Secretary of State that, for reasons stated in my telegram of 1st August, I most earnestly trust that the orders already sent to Hamburg to allow the clearance of British ships covers also the release of their cargoes, the detention of which cannot be justified.

Sir E. Goschen, British Ambassador at Berlin, to Sir Edward Grey.—(Received August 3.)
(Telegraphic.)   Berlin, August 3, 1914.

YOUR telegram of 2nd August: Detention of British ships at Hamburg.

No information available.

Sir F. Villiers, British Minister at Brussels, to Sir Edward Grey.—(Received August 3.)
(Telegraphic.)   Brussels, August 3, 1914.

FRENCH Government have offered through their military attaché the support of five French army corps to the Belgian Government. Following reply has been sent to-day:—

"We are sincerely grateful to the French Government for offering eventual support. In the actual circumstances, however, we do not propose to appeal to the guarantee of the Powers. Belgian Government will decide later on the action which they may think it necessary to take."

Sir Edward Grey to Sir F. Bertie, British Ambassador at Paris.

Sir,   Foreign Office, August 3, 1914.

ON the 1st instant the French Ambassador made the following communication:—

"In reply to the German Government's intimation of the fact that ultimatums had been presented to France and Russia, and to the question as to what were the intentions of Italy, the Marquis di San Giuliano replied:—

"'The war undertaken by Austria, and the consequences which might result, had, in the words of the German Ambassador himself, an aggressive object. Both were therefore in conflict with the purely defensive character of the Triple Alliance, and in such circumstances Italy would remain neutral.'"

In making this communication, M. Cambon was instructed to lay stress upon the Italian declaration that the present war was not a defensive but an aggressive war, and that, for this reason, the *casus fœderis* under the terms of the Triple Alliance did not arise.

I am, &c.

E. GREY.

Sir Edward Grey to Sir E. Goschen, British Ambassador at Berlin.

(Telegraphic.)   Foreign Office, August 4, 1914.

THE King of the Belgians has made an appeal to His Majesty the King for diplomatic intervention on behalf of Belgium in the following terms:—

"Remembering the numerous proofs of your Majesty's friendship and that of your predecessor, and the friendly attitude of England in 1870 and the proof of friendship you have just given us again, I make a supreme appeal to the diplomatic intervention of your Majesty's Government to safeguard the integrity of Belgium."

His Majesty's Government are also informed that the German Government have delivered to the Belgian Government a note proposing friendly neutrality entailing free passage through Belgian territory, and promising to maintain the independence and integrity of the kingdom and its possessions at the conclusion of peace, threatening in case of refusal to treat Belgium as an enemy. An answer was requested within twelve hours.

We also understand that Belgium has categorically refused this as a flagrant violation of the law of nations.

His Majesty's Government are bound to protest against this violation of a treaty to which Germany is a party in common with themselves, and must request an assurance that the demand made upon. Belgium will not be proceeded with and that her neutrality will be respected by Germany. You should ask for an immediate reply.

Sir F. Villiers, British Minister at Brussels, to Sir Edward Grey.—(Received August 4.)

(Telegraphic.)   Brussels, August 4, 1914.

GERMAN Minister has this morning addressed note to Minister for Foreign Affairs stating that as Belgian Government have declined the well-intentioned proposals submitted to them by the Imperial Government, the latter will, deeply to their regret, be compelled to carry out, if necessary by force of arms, the measures considered indispensable in view of the French menaces.

Sir Edward Grey to Sir F. Villiers, British Minister at Brussels.

(Telegraphic.)   Foreign Office, August 4, 1914.

YOU should inform Belgian Government that if pressure is applied to them by Germany to induce them to depart from neutrality, His Majesty's Government expect that they will resist by any means in their power, and that His Majesty's Government will support them in offering such resistance, and that His Majesty's Government in this event are prepared to join Russia and France, if desired, in offering to the Belgian Government at once common action for the purpose of resisting use of force by Germany against them, and a guarantee to maintain their independence and integrity in future years.

Sir Edward Grey to Sir E. Goschen, British Ambassador at Berlin.
(Telegraphic.)   Foreign Office, August 4, 1914.

I CONTINUE to receive numerous complaints from British firms as to the detention of their ships at Hamburg, Cuxhaven, and other German ports. This action on the part of the German authorities is totally unjustifiable. It is in direct contravention of international law and of the assurances given to your Excellency by the Imperial Chancellor. You should demand the immediate release of all British ships if such release has not yet been given.

German Foreign Secretary to Prince Lichnowsky, German Ambassador in London.—(Communicated by German Embassy, August 4.)
(Telegraphic.)   Berlin, August 4, 1914.

PLEASE dispel any mistrust that may subsist on the part of the British Government with regard to our intentions, by repeating most positively formal assurance that, even in the case of armed conflict with Belgium, Germany will, under no pretence whatever, annex Belgian territory. Sincerity of this declaration is borne out by fact that we solemnly pledged our word to Holland strictly to respect her neutrality. It is obvious that we could not profitably annex Belgian territory without making at the same time territorial acquisitions at expense of Holland. Please impress upon Sir E. Grey that German army could not be exposed to French attack across Belgium, which was planned according to absolutely unimpeachable information. Germany had consequently to disregard Belgian neutrality, it being for her a question of life or death to prevent French advance.

Sir F. Villiers, British Minister at Brussels, to Sir Edward Grey.—(Received August 4.)
(Telegraphic.)   Brussels, August 4, 1914.

MILITARY attaché has been informed at War Office that German troops have entered Belgian territory, and that Liège has been summoned to surrender by small party of Germans who, however, were repulsed.

Sir Edward Grey to Sir E. Goschen, British Ambassador at Berlin.
(Telegraphic.)   Foreign Office, August 4, 1914.

WE hear that Germany has addressed note to Belgian Minister for Foreign Affairs stating that German Government will be compelled to carry out, if necessary, by force of arms, the measures considered indispensable.

We are also informed that Belgian territory has been violated at Gemmenich.

In these circumstances, and in view of the fact that Germany declined to give the same assurance respecting Belgium as France gave last week in reply to our request made simultaneously at Berlin and Paris, we must repeat that request, and ask that a satisfactory reply to it and to my telegram of this morning be received here by 12 o'clock to-night. If not, you are instructed to ask for your passports, and to say that His Majesty's Government feel bound to take all steps in their power to uphold the neutrality of Belgium and the observance of a treaty to which Germany is as much a party as ourselves.

GERMANY AND BRITAIN

Sir E. Goschen, British Ambassador in Berlin, to Sir Edward Grey.

Sir,   London, August 8, 1914.

IN accordance with the instructions contained in your telegram of the 4th instant I called upon the Secretary of State that afternoon and enquired, in the name of His Majesty's Government, whether the Imperial Government would refrain from violating Belgian neutrality. Herr von Jagow at once replied that he was sorry to say that his answer must be "No," as, in consequence of the German troops having crossed the frontier that morning, Belgian neutrality had been already violated. Herr von Jagow again went into the reasons why the Imperial Government had been obliged to take this step, namely, that they had to advance into France by the quickest and easiest way, so as to be able to get well ahead with their operations and endeavour to strike some decisive blow as early as possible. It was a matter of life and death for them, as if they had gone by the more southern route they could not have hoped, in view of the paucity of roads and the strength of the fortresses, to have got through without formidable opposition entailing great loss of time. This loss of time would have meant time gained by the Russians for bringing up their troops to the German frontier. Rapidity of action was the great German asset, while that of Russia was an inexhaustible supply of troops. I pointed out to Herr von Jagow that this *fait accompli* of the violation of the Belgian frontier rendered, as he would readily understand, the situation exceedingly grave, and I asked him whether there was not still time to draw back and avoid possible consequences, which both he and I would deplore. He replied that, for the reasons he had given me, it was now impossible for them to draw back.

During the afternoon I received your further telegram of the same date, and, in compliance with the instructions therein contained, I again proceeded to the Imperial Foreign Office and informed the Secretary of State that unless the Imperial Government could give the assurance by 12 o'clock that night that they would proceed no further with their violation of the Belgian frontier and stop their advance, I had been instructed to demand my passports and inform the Imperial Government that His Majesty's Government would have to take all steps in their power to uphold the neutrality of Belgium and the observance of a treaty to which Germany was as much a party as themselves.

Herr von Jagow replied that to his great regret he could give no other answer than that which he had given me earlier in the day, namely, that the safety of the Empire rendered it absolutely necessary that the Imperial troops should advance through Belgium. I gave his Excellency a written summary of your telegram and, pointing out that you had mentioned 12 o'clock as the time when His Majesty's Government would expect an answer, asked him whether, in view of the terrible consequences which would necessarily ensue, it were not possible even at the last moment that their answer should be reconsidered. He replied that if the time given were even twenty-four hours or more, his answer must be the same. I said that in that case I should have to demand my passports. This interview took place at about 7 o'clock. In a short conversation which ensued Herr von Jagow expressed his poignant regret at the crumbling of his entire policy and that of the Chancellor, which had been to make friends with Great Britain, and then, through Great Britain, to get closer to France. I said that this sudden end to my work in Berlin was to me also a matter of deep regret and disappointment, but that he must understand that under the circumstances and in view of our engagements, His Majesty's Government could not possibly have acted otherwise than they had done.

I then said that I should like to go and see the Chancellor, as it might be, perhaps, the last time I should have an opportunity of seeing him. He begged me to do so. I found the Chancellor very agitated. His Excellency at once began a harangue, which lasted for about twenty minutes. He said that the step taken by His Majesty's Government was terrible to a degree; just for a word—"neutrality," a word which in war time had so often been disregarded—just for a scrap of paper Great Britain was going to make war on a kindred nation who desired nothing better than to be friends with her. All his efforts in that direction had been rendered useless by this last terrible step, and the policy to which, as I knew, he had devoted himself since his accession to office had tumbled down like a house of cards. What we had done was unthinkable; it was like striking a man from behind while he was fighting for his life against two assailants. He held Great Britain responsible for all the terrible events that might happen. I protested strongly against that statement, and said that, in the same way as he and Herr von Jagow wished me to understand that for strategical reasons it was a matter of life and death to Germany to advance through Belgium and violate the latter's neutrality, so I would wish him to understand that it was, so to speak, a matter of "life and death" for the honour of Great Britain that she should keep her solemn engagement to do her utmost to defend Belgium's neutrality if attacked. That solemn compact simply had to be kept, or what confidence could anyone have in engagements given by Great Britain in the future? The Chancellor said, "But at what price will that compact have been kept. Has the British Government thought of that?" I hinted to his Excellency as plainly as I could that fear of consequences could hardly be regarded as an excuse for breaking solemn engagements, but his Excellency was so excited, so evidently overcome by the news of our action, and so little disposed to hear reason that I refrained from adding fuel to the flame by further argument. As I was leaving he said that the blow of Great Britain joining Germany's enemies was all the greater that almost up to the last moment he and his Government had been working with us and supporting our efforts to maintain peace between Austria and Russia. I said that this was part of the tragedy which saw the two nations fall apart just at the moment when the relations between them had been more friendly and cordial than they had been for years. Unfortunately, notwithstanding our efforts to maintain peace between Russia and Austria, the war had spread and had brought us face to face with a situation which, if we held to our engagements, we could not possibly avoid, and which unfortunately entailed our separation from our late fellow-workers. He would readily understand that no one regretted this more than I.

After this somewhat painful interview I returned to the embassy and drew up a telegraphic report of what had passed. This telegram was handed in at the Central Telegraph Office a little before 9 P.M. It was accepted by that office, but apparently never despatched.

At about 9.30 P.M. Herr von Zimmermann, the Under-Secretary of State, came to see me. After expressing his deep regret that the very friendly official and personal relations between us were about to cease, he asked me casually whether a demand for passports was equivalent to a declaration of war. I said that such an authority on international law as he was known to be must know as well or better than I what was usual in such cases. I added that there were many cases where diplomatic relations had been broken off, and, nevertheless, war had not ensued; but that in this case he would have seen from my instructions, of which I had given Herr von Jagow a written summary, that His Majesty's Government expected an answer to a definite question by 12 o'clock that night and that in default of a satisfactory answer they would be forced to take such steps as their engagements required. Herr Zimmermann said that that was, in fact, a declaration of war, as the Imperial Government could not possibly give the assurance required either that night or any other night.

In the meantime, after Herr Zimmermann left me, a flying sheet, issued by the "Berliner Tageblatt," was circulated stating that Great Britain had declared war against Germany. The immediate result of this news was the assemblage of an exceedingly excited and unruly mob before His Majesty's Embassy. The small force of police which had been sent to guard the embassy was soon overpowered, and the attitude of the mob became more threatening. We took no notice of this demonstration as long as it was confined to noise, but when the crash of glass and the landing of cobble stones into the drawingroom, where we were all sitting, warned us that the situation was getting unpleasant, I telephoned to the Foreign Office an account of what was happening. Herr von Jagow at once informed the Chief of Police, and an adequate force of mounted police, sent with great promptness, very soon cleared the street. From that moment on we were well guarded, and no more direct unpleasantness occurred.

After order had been restored Herr von Jagow came to see me and expressed his most heartfelt regrets at what had occurred. He said that the behaviour of his countrymen had made him feel more ashamed than he had words to express. It was an indelible stain on the reputation of Berlin. He said that the flying sheet circulated in the streets had not been authorised by the Government; in fact, the Chancellor had asked him by telephone whether he thought that such a statement should be issued, and he had replied, "Certainly not, until the morning." It was in consequence of his decision to that effect that only a small force of police had been sent to the neighbourhood of the embassy, as he had thought that the presence of a large force would inevitably attract attention and perhaps lead to disturbances. It was the "pestilential 'Tageblatt,' " which had somehow got hold of the news, that had upset his calculations. He had heard rumours that the mob had been excited to violence by gestures made and missiles thrown from the embassy, but he felt sure that that was not true (I was able soon to assure him that the report had no foundation whatever), and even if it was, it was no excuse for the disgraceful scenes which had taken place. He feared that I would take home with me a sorry impression of Berlin manners in moments of excitement. In fact, no apology could have been more full and complete.

On the following morning, the 5th August, the Emperor sent one of His Majesty's aides-de-camp to me with the following message:-

"The Emperor has charged me to express to your Excellency his regret for the occurrences of last night, but to tell you at the same time that you will gather from those occurrences an idea of the feelings of his people respecting the action of Great Britain in join-ing with other nations against her old allies of Waterloo. His Majesty also begs that you will tell the King that he has been proud of the titles of British Field-Marshal and British Admiral, but that in conse-quence of what has occurred he must now at once divest himself of those titles."

I would add that the above message lost none of its acerbity by the manner of its delivery.

On the other hand, I should like to state that I received all through this trying time nothing but

courtesy at the hands of Herr von Jagow and the officials of the Imperial Foreign Office. At about 11
o'clock on the same morning Count Wedel handed
me my passports—which I had earlier in the day
demanded in writing—and told me that he had been
instructed to confer with me as to the route which I
should follow for my return to England. He said that
he had understood that I preferred the route viâ the
Hook of Holland to that viâ Copenhagen; they had
therefore arranged that I should go by the former
route, only I should have to wait till the following
morning. I agreed to this, and he said that I might be
quite assured that there would be no repetition of the
disgraceful scenes of the preceding night as full precautions would be taken. He added that they were
doing all in their power to have a restaurant car
attached to the train, but it was rather a difficult matter. He also brought me a charming letter from Herr
von Jagow couched in the most friendly terms. The
day was passed in packing up such articles as time
allowed.

The night passed quietly without any incident. In
the morning a strong force of police was posted along
the usual route to the Lehrter Station, while the
embassy was smuggled away in taxi-cabs to the station
by side streets. We there suffered no molestation
whatever, and avoided the treatment meted out by
the crowd to my Russian and French colleagues.
Count Wedel met us at the station to say good-bye on
behalf of Herr von Jagow and to see that all the
arrangements ordered for our comfort had been

properly carried out. A retired colonel of the Guards accompanied the train to the Dutch frontier and was exceedingly kind in his efforts to prevent the great crowds which thronged the platforms at every station where we stopped from insulting us; but beyond the yelling of patriotic songs and a few jeers and insulting gestures we had really nothing to complain of during our tedious journey to the Dutch frontier.

Before closing this long account of our last days in Berlin I should like to place on record and bring to your notice the quite admirable behaviour of my staff under the most trying circumstances possible. One and all, they worked night and day with scarcely any rest, and I cannot praise too highly the cheerful zeal with which counsellor, naval and military attachés, secretaries, and the two young attachés buckled to their work and kept their nerve with often a yelling mob outside and inside hundreds of British subjects clamouring for advice and assistance. I was proud to have such a staff to work with, and feel most grateful to them all for the invaluable assistance and support, often exposing them to considerable personal risk, which they so readily and cheerfully gave to me.

I should also like to mention the great assistance rendered to us all by my American colleague, Mr. Gerard, and his staff. Undeterred by the hooting and hisses with which he was often greeted by the mob on entering and leaving the embassy, his Excellency came repeatedly to see me to ask how he could help us and to make arrangements for the safety of stranded British subjects. He extricated many of these from extremely difficult situations at some personal risk to himself, and his calmness and *savoir-faire* and his firmness in dealing with the Imperial authorities gave full assurance that the protection of British subjects and interests could not have been left in more efficient and able hands.

I have, &c.

W. E. GOSCHEN.

From M Cambon, French Ambassador in Berlin, to Herr von Jagow

Berlin   August 4 1914

Sir,

More than once your Excellency has said to me that the Imperial Government, in accordance with the usages of international courtesy, would facilitate my return to my own country and would give me every means of getting back to it quickly.

Yesterday, however, Baron von Langworth, after refusing me access to Belgium and Holland, informed me that I should travel to Switzerland via Constance. During the night I was informed that I should be sent to Austria, a country which is taking part in the present war on the side of Germany. As I had no knowledge of the intentions of Austria towards me, since on Austrian soil I am nothing but an ordinary private individual, I wrote to Baron von Langwerth that I requested the Imperial Government to give me a promise that the Imperial and Royal Austrian authorities would give me all possible facilities for continuing my journey and that Switzerland would not be closed to me. Herr von Langwerth has been good enough to answer me in writing that I could be assured of an easy journey and that the Austrian authorities would do all that was necessary.

It is nearly five o'clock and Baron von Langwerth has just announced to me that I shall be sent to Denmark. In view of the present situation there is no security that I shall find a ship to England and it is this consideration which made me reject this proposal with the approval of Herr von Langwerth.

Extract from M. Cambon's report to the French Government.

Whilst my letter was being delivered I was told that the journey would not be made direct but by way of Schleswig. At 10 o'clock in the evening, I left the Embassy with my staff in the middle of a great assembly of foot and mounted police.

At the station the Ministry of Foreign Affairs was only represented by an officer of inferior rank.

The journey took place with extreme slowness. We took more than twenty four hours to reach the frontier. It seemed that at every station they had to wait for orders to proceed. I was accompanied by Major von Rheinbaben of The Alexandra Regiment of the Guard and by a police officer. In the neighbourhood of the Kiel Canal the soldiers entered our carriage. The windows were shut and the curtains of the carriages drawn down; each of us had to remain isolated in his compartment and was forbidden to get up or to touch his luggage. A soldier stood in the carriage before the door of each of our compartments which were kept open, revolver in hand anf finger on the trigger. The Russian Charge d'Affaires, the women and children and everyone were subjected to the same treatment.

At the last German station about 11 o' clock at night, Major vin Rheinbaben came to take leave of me. I handed him a letter for Herr von Jagow which included the following remarks.

"Today as the train in which I was passed over the Kiel Canal an attempt was made to search all our luggage as if we might have hidden some instrument of destruction. Thanks to the interference of Major von Rheinbaben we were spared this insult. Yesterday I had the honour of writing to your Excellency that I was being treated almost as a prisoner. Today I am being treated as a dangerous prisoner. Also I must record that during our journey which from Berlin to Denmark has taken twenty-four hours, no food has been prepared nor provided for me nor for the persons who were travelling with me to the frontier."

I thought that our troubles were finished, when shortly afterwards Major von Rheinbaben came, rather embarrassed, to inform me that the train would not proceed to the Danish frontier if I did not pay the cost of this train. I expressed my astonishment that I had not been made to pay at Berlin and that at any rate I had not been forewarned of this. I offered to pay by a cheque on one of the largest Berlin banks. This facility was refused me. With the help of my companions I was able to collect, in gold, the sum which was required from me at once, and which amounted to 3,611 marks 75 pfennig. This is about 5,000 francs at the present rate of exchange.

I am assured that my British colleague and the Belgian minister, although they left Berlin after I did, travelled by the direct route to Holland. I am struck by this difference of treatment, and as Denmark and Norway are, at this moment infested with spies, if I succeed in embarking in Norway, there is a danger that I may be arrested at sea with the officials who accompany me.

I do not wish to conclude this despatch wothout notifying your Excellency of the energy and devotion of which the whole staff of the Embassy has given unceasing proof during the course of this crisis. I shall be glad that this account should be taken of the services which on this occasion have been rendered to the Government of the Republic, in particular by the Secretaries of the Embassy and by the Military and Naval Attaches.

JULES CAMBON

Vienna

Sir M. de Bunsen, British Ambassador in Vienna, to Sir Edward Grey.

Sir,   London, September 1, 1914.

THE rapidity of the march of events during the days which led up to the outbreak of the European war made it difficult, at the time, to do more than record their progress by telegraph. I propose now to add a few comments.

The delivery at Belgrade on the 23rd July of the Austrian note to Serbia was preceded by a period of absolute silence at the Ballplatz. Except Herr von Tschirscky, who must have been aware of the tenour, if not of the actual words of the note, none of my colleagues were allowed to see through the veil. On the 22nd and 23rd July, M. Dumaine, French Ambassador, had long interviews with Baron Macchio, one of the Under-Secretaries of State for Foreign Affairs, by whom he was left under the impression that the words of warning he had been instructed to speak to the Austro-Hungarian Government had not been unavailing, and that the note which was being drawn up would be found to contain nothing with which a self-respecting State need hesitate to comply. At the second of these interviews he was not even informed that the note was at that very moment being presented at Belgrade, or that it would be published in Vienna on the following morning. Count Forgach, the other Under-Secretary of State, had indeed been good enough to confide to me on the same day the true character of the note, and the fact of its presentation about the time we were speaking.

So little had the Russian Ambassador been made aware of what was preparing that he actually left Vienna on a fortnight's leave of absence about the

20th July. He had only been absent a few days when events compelled him to return. It might have been supposed that Duke Avarna, Ambassador of the allied Italian Kingdom, which was bound to be so closely affected by fresh complications in the Balkans, would have been taken fully into the confidence of Count Berchtold during this critical time. In point of fact his Excellency was left completely in the dark. As for myself, no indication was given me by Count Berchtold of the impending storm, and it was from a private source that I received on the 15th July the forecast of what was about to happen which I telegraphed to you the following day. It is true that during all this time the "Neue Freie Presse" and other leading Viennese newspapers were using language which pointed unmistakably to war with Serbia. The official "Fremdenblatt," however, was more cautious, and till the note was published, the prevailing opinion among my colleagues was that Austria would shrink from courses calculated to involve her in grave European complications.

On the 24th July the note was published in the newspapers. By common consent it was at once styled an ultimatum. Its integral acceptance by Serbia was neither expected nor desired, and when, on the following afternoon, it was at first rumoured in Vienna that it had been unconditionally accepted, there was a moment of keen disappointment. The mistake was quickly corrected, and as soon as it was known later in the evening that the Serbian reply had been rejected and that Baron Giesl had broken off relations at Belgrade, Vienna burst into a frenzy of delight, vast crowds parading the streets and singing patriotic songs till the small hours of the morning.

The demonstrations were perfectly orderly, consisting for the most part of organised processions through the principal streets ending up at the Ministry of War. One or two attempts to make hostile manifestations against the Russian Embassy were frustrated by the strong guard of police which held the approaches to the principal embassies during those days. The demeanour of the people at Vienna and, as I was informed, in many other principal cities of the Monarchy, showed plainly the popularity of the idea of war with Serbia, and there can be no doubt that the small body of Austrian and Hungarian statesmen by whom this momentous step was adopted gauged rightly the sense, and it may even be said the determination, of the people, except presumably in portions of the provinces inhabited by the Slav races. There had been much disappointment in many quarters at the avoidance of war with Serbia during the annexation crisis in 1908 and again in connection with the recent Balkan war. Count Berchtold's peace policy had met with little sympathy in the Delegation. Now the flood-gates were opened, and the entire people and press clamoured impatiently for immediate and condign punishment of the hated Serbian race. The country certainly believed that it had before it only the alternative of subduing Serbia or of submitting sooner or later to mutilation at her hands. But a peaceful solution should first have been

attempted. Few seemed to reflect that the forcible
intervention of a Great Power in the Balkans must
inevitably call other Great Powers into the field. So
just was the cause of Austria held to be, that it seemed
to her people inconceivable that any country should
place itself in her path, or that questions of mere policy or prestige should be regarded anywhere as
superseding the necessity which had arisen to exact
summary vengeance for the crime of Serajevo. The
conviction had been expressed to me by the German
Ambassador on the 24th July that Russia would stand
aside. This feeling, which was also held at the
Ballplatz, influenced no doubt the course of events,
and it is deplorable that no effort should have been
made to secure by means of diplomatic negotiations
the acquiescence of Russia and Europe as a whole in
some peaceful compromise of the Serbian question
by which Austrian fears of Serbian aggression and
intrigue might have been removed for the future.
Instead of adopting this course the Austro-Hungarian
Government resolved upon war. The inevitable consequence ensued. Russia replied to a partial Austrian
mobilisation and declaration of war against Serbia by
a partial Russian mobilisation against Austria. Austria
met this move by completing her own mobilisation,
and Russia again responded with results which have
passed into history. The fate of the proposals put forward by His Majesty's Government for the
preservation of peace is recorded in the White Paper
on the European Crisis. On the 28th July I saw
Count Berchtold and urged as strongly as I could that

the scheme of mediation mentioned in your speech in the House of Commons on the previous day should be accepted as offering an honourable and peaceful settlement of the question at issue. His Excellency himself read to me a telegraphic report of the speech, but added that matters had gone too far; Austria was that day declaring war on Serbia, and she could never accept the conference which you had suggested should take place between the less interested Powers on the basis of the Serbian reply. This was a mater which must be settled directly between the two parties immediately concerned. I said His Majesty's Government would hear with regret that hostilities could not be arrested, as you feared they would lead to European complications. I disclaimed any British lack of sympathy with Austria in the matter of her legitimate grievances against Serbia, and pointed out that whereas Austria seemed to be making these the starting point of her policy, His Majesty's Government were bound to look at the question primarily from the point of view of the maintenance of the peace of Europe. In this way the two countries might easily drift apart.

His Excellency said that he too was keeping the European aspect of the question in sight. He thought, however, that Russia would have no right to intervene after receiving his assurance that Austria sought no territorial aggrandisement. His Excellency remarked to me in the course of his conversation that, though he had been glad to co-operate towards bringing about the settlement which had resulted from the ambassadorial conferences in London during the Balkan crisis, he had never had much belief in the permanency of that settlement, which was necessarily of a highly artificial character, inasmuch as the interests which it sought to harmonise were in themselves profoundly divergent. His Excellency maintained a most friendly demeanour throughout the interview, but left no doubt in my mind as to the determination of the Austro-Hungarian Government to proceed with the invasion of Serbia.

The German Government claim to have persevered to the end in the endeavour to support at Vienna your successive proposals in the interest of peace. Herr von Tschirscky abstained from inviting my co-operation or that of the French and Russian Ambassadors in carrying out his instructions to that effect, and I had no means of knowing what response he was receiving from the Austro-Hungarian Government. I was, however, kept fully informed by M. Schebeko, the Russian Ambassador, of his own direct negotiations with Count Berchtold. M. Schebeko endeavoured on the 28th July to persuade the Austro-Hungarian Government to furnish Count Szapary with full powers to continue at St. Petersburgh the hopeful conversations which had there been taking place between the latter and M. Sazonof. Count Berchtold refused at the time, but two days later (30th July), though in the meantime Russia had partially mobilised against Austria, he received M. Schebeko again, in a perfectly friendly manner, and gave his consent to the continuance of the conversations at St. Petersburgh. From now onwards the tension between Russia and Germany was much greater than between Russia and Austria. As between the latter an arrangement seemed almost in sight, and on the 1st August I was informed by M. Schebeko that Count Szapary had at last conceded the main point at issue by announcing to M. Sazonof that Austria would consent to submit to mediation the points in the note to Serbia which seemed incompatible with the maintenance of Serbian independence. M. Sazonof, M. Schebeko added, had accepted this proposal on condition that Austria would refrain from the actual invasion of Serbia. Austria, in fact, had finally yielded, and that she herself had at this point good hopes of a peaceful issue is shown by the communication made to you on the 1st August by Count Mensdorff, to the effect that Austria had neither "banged the door" on compromise nor cut off the conversations. M. Schebeko to the end was working hard for peace. He was holding the most conciliatory language to Count Berchtold, and he informed me that the latter, as well as Count Forgach, had responded in the same spirit. Certainly it was too much for Russia to expect that Austria would hold back her armies, but this matter could probably have been settled by negotiation, and M. Schebeko repeatedly told me he was prepared to accept any reasonable compromise.

Unfortunately these conversations at St. Petersburgh and Vienna were cut short by the transfer of the dispute to the more dangerous ground of a direct conflict between Germany and Russia. Germany intervened on the 31st July by means of her double ultimatums to St. Petersburgh and Paris. The ultimatums were of a kind to which only one answer is possible, and Germany declared war on Russia on the 1st August, and on France on the 3rd August. A few days' delay might in all probability have saved Europe from one of the greatest calamities in history.

Russia still abstained from attacking Austria, and M. Schebeko had been instructed to remain at his post till war should actually be declared against her by the Austro-Hungarian Government. This only happened on the 6th August when Count Berchtold informed the foreign missions at Vienna that "the Austro-Hungarian Ambassador at St. Petersburgh had been instructed to notify the Russian Government that, in view of the menacing attitude of Russia in the Austro-Serbian conflict and the fact that Russia had commenced hostilities against Germany, Austria-Hungary considered herself also at war with Russia."

M. Schebeko left quietly in a special train provided by the Austro-Hungarian Government on the 7th August. He had urgently requested to be conveyed to the Roumanian frontier, so that he might be able to proceed to his own country, but was taken instead to the Swiss frontier, and ten days later I found him at Berne.

M. Dumaine, French Ambassador, stayed on till the 12th August. On the previous day he had been instructed to demand his passport on the ground that

Austrian troops were being employed against France. This point was not fully cleared up when I left Vienna. On the 9th August, M. Dumaine had received from Count Berchtold the categorical declaration that no Austrian troops were being moved to Alsace. The next day this statement was supplemented by a further one, in writing, giving Count Berchtold's assurance that not only had no Austrian troops been moved actually to the French frontier, but that none were moving from Austria in a westerly direction into Germany in such a way that they might replace German troops employed at the front. These two statements were made by Count Berchtold in reply to precise questions put to him by M. Dumaine, under instructions from his Government. The French Ambassador's departure was not attended by any hostile demonstration, but his Excellency before leaving had been justly offended by a harangue made by the Chief Burgomaster of Vienna to the crowd assembled before the steps of the town hall, in which he assured the people that Paris was in the throes of a revolution, and that the President of the Republic had been assassinated.

The British declaration of war on Germany was made known in Vienna by special editions of the newspapers about midday on the 4th August. An abstract of your speeches in the House of Commons, and also of the German Chancellor's speech in the Reichstag of the 4th August, appeared the same day, as well as the text of the German ultimatum to Belgium. Otherwise few details of the great events of these days transpired. The "Neue Freie Presse" was violently insulting towards England. The "Fremdenblatt" was not offensive, but little or nothing was said in the columns of any Vienna paper to explain that the violation of Belgium neutrality had left His Majesty's Government no alternative but to take part in the war.

The declaration of Italian neutrality was bitterly felt in Vienna, but scarcely mentioned in the newspapers.

On the 5th August I had the honour to receive your instruction of the previous day preparing me for the immediate outbreak of war with Germany, but adding that, Austria being understood to be not yet at that date at war with Russia and France, you did not desire me to ask for my passport or to make any particular communication to the Austro-Hungarian Government. You stated at the same time that His Majesty's Government of course expected Austria not to commit any act of war against us without the notice required by diplomatic usage.

On Thursday morning, the 13th August, I had the honour to receive your telegram of the 12th, stating that you had been compelled to inform Count Mensdorff, at the request of the French Government, that a complete rupture had occurred between France and Austria, on the ground that Austria had declared war on Russia who was already fighting on the side of France, and that Austria had sent troops to the German frontier under conditions that were a direct menace to France. The rupture having been brought about with France in this way, I was to ask for my passport, and your telegram stated, in conclusion, that you had informed Count Mensdorff that a state of war would exist between the two countries from midnight of the 12th August.

After seeing Mr. Penfield, the United States Ambassador, who accepted immediately in the most friendly spirit my request that his Excellency would take charge provisionally of British interests in Austria-Hungary during the unfortunate interruption of relations, I proceeded, with Mr. Theo Russell, Counsellor of His Majesty's Embassy, to the Ballplatz. Count Berchtold received me at midday. I delivered my message, for which his Excellency did not seem to be unprepared, although he told me that a long telegram from Count Mensdorff had just come in but had not yet been brought to him. His Excellency received my communication with the courtesy which never leaves him. He deplored the unhappy complications which were drawing such good friends as Austria and England into war. In point of fact, he added, Austria did not consider herself then at war with France, though diplomatic relations with that country had been broken off. I explained in a few words how circumstances had forced this unwelcome conflict upon us. We both avoided useless argument. Then I ventured to recommend to his Excellency's consideration the case of the numerous stranded British subjects at Carlsbad, Vienna, and other places throughout the country. I had already had some correspondence with him on the subject, and his

Excellency took a note of what I said, and promised
to see what could be done to get them away when
the stress of mobilisation should be over. Count
Berchtold agreed to Mr. Phillpotts, till then British
consul at Vienna under Consul-General Sir Frederick
Duncan, being left by me at the Embassy in the
capacity of Chargé des Archives. He presumed a similar privilege would not be refused in England if
desired on behalf of the Austro-Hungarian
Government. I took leave of Count Berchtold with
sincere regret, having received from the day of my
arrival in Vienna, not quite nine months before, many
marks of friendship and consideration from his
Excellency. As I left I begged his Excellency to present my profound respects to the Emperor Francis
Joseph, together with an expression of my hope that
His Majesty would pass through these sad times with
unimpaired health and strength. Count Berchtold was
pleased to say he would deliver my message.

Count Walterskirchen, of the Austro-Hungarian
Foreign Office, was deputed the following morning
to bring me my passport and to acquaint me with the
arrangements made for my departure that evening
(14th August). In the course of the day Countess
Berchtold and other ladies of Vienna society called to
take leave of Lady de Bunsen at the embassy. We left
the railway station by special train for the Swiss frontier at 7 p.m. No disagreeable incidents occurred,
Count Walterskirchen was present at the station on
behalf of Count Berchtold. The journey was necessarily slow, owing to the encumbered state of the line.

We reached Buchs, on the Swiss frontier, early in the morning of the 17th August. At the first halting place there had been some hooting and stone throwing on the part of the entraining troops and station officials, but no inconvenience was caused, and at the other large stations on our route we found that ample measures had been taken to preserve us from molestation as well as to provide us with food. I was left in no doubt that the Austro-Hungarian Government had desired that the journey should be performed under the most comfortable conditions possible, and that I should receive on my departure all the marks of consideration due to His Majesty's representative. I was accompanied by my own family and the entire staff of the embassy, for whose untiring zeal and efficient help in trying times I desire to express my sincere thanks. The Swiss Government also showed courtesy in providing comfortable accommodation during our journey from the frontier to Berne, and, after three days' stay there, on to Geneva, at which place we found that every provision had been made by the French Government, at the request of Sir Francis Bertie, for our speedy conveyance to Paris. We reached England on Saturday morning, the 22nd August.

I have, &c.

MAURICE DE BUNSEN.

Other titles in the series

John Profumo and Christine Keeler, 1963

"The story must start with Stephen Ward, aged fifty. The son of a clergymen, by profession he was an osteopath ... his skill was very considerable and he included among his patients many well-known people ...Yet at the same time he was utterly immoral."

The Backdrop

The beginning of the '60s saw the publication of 'Lady Chatterley's Lover' and the dawn of sexual and social liberation as traditional morals began to be questioned and in some instances swept away.

The Book

In spite of the spiralling spate of recent political falls from grace, The Profumo Affair remains the biggest scandal ever to hit British politics. The Minister of War was found to be having an affair with a call girl who had associations with a Russian Naval Officer at the height of the Cold War. There are questions of cover-up, lies told to Parliament, bribery and stories sold to the newspapers. Lord Denning's superbly written report into the scandal describes with astonishment and fascinated revulsion the extraordinary sexual behaviour of the ruling classes. Orgies, naked bathing, sado-masochistic gatherings of the great and good and ministers and judges cavorting in masks are all uncovered.

ISBN 0 11 702402 3

The Loss of the Titanic, 1912

"From 'Mesabe' to 'Titanic' and all east bound ships. Ice report in Latitude 42N to 41.25N; Longitude 49 to 50.30W. Saw much Heavy Pack Ice and a great number of Large Icebergs. Also Field Ice. Weather good. Clear."

The Backdrop

The watchwords were 'bigger, better, faster, more luxurious' as builders of ocean-going vessels strove to outdo each other as they raced to capitalise on a new golden age of travel.

The Book

The story of the sinking of the Titanic, as told by the official enquiry, reveals some remarkable facts which have been lost in popular re-tellings of the story. A ship of the same line, only a few miles away from the Titanic as she sank, should have been able to rescue passengers, so why did this not happen? Readers of this fascinating report will discover that many such questions remain unanswered and that the full story of a tragedy which has entered into popular mythology has by no means been told.

ISBN 0 11 702403 1

Tragedy at Bethnal Green, 1943

"Immediately the alert was sounded a large number of people left their houses in the utmost haste for shelter. A great many were running. Two cinemas at least in the near vicinity disgorged a large number of people and at least three omnibuses set down their passengers outside the shelter."

The Backdrop

The beleaguered East End of London had born much of the brunt of the Blitz but, in 1943, four years into WW2, it seemed that the worst of the bombing was over.

The Book

The new unfinished tube station at Bethnal Green was one of the largest air raid shelters in London. After a warning siren sounded on March 3, 1943, there was a rush to the shelter. By 8.20pm, a matter of minutes after the alarm had sounded, 174 people lay dead, crushed trying to get into the tube station's booking hall. At the official enquiry, questions were asked about the behaviour of certain officials and whether the accident could have been prevented.

ISBN 0 11 702404 X

The Judgement of Nuremberg, 1946

"Efficient and enduring intimidation can only be achieved either by Capital Punishment or by measures by which the relatives of the criminal and the population do not know the fate of the criminal. This aim is achieved when the criminal is transferred to Germany."

The Backdrop

WW2 is over, there is a climate of jubilation and optimism as the Allies look to rebuilding Europe for the future but the perpetrators of Nazi War Crimes have yet to be reckoned with, and the full extent of their atrocities is as yet widely unknown.

The Book

Today, we have lived with the full knowledge of the extent of Nazi atrocities for over half a century and yet they still retain their power to shock. Imagine what it was like as they were being revealed in the full extent of their horror for the first time. In this book the Judges at the Nuremberg Trials take it in turn to describe the indictments handed down to the defendants and their crimes. The entire history, purpose and method of the Nazi party since its foundation in 1918 is revealed and described in chilling detail.

ISBN 0 11 702406 6

The Boer War: Ladysmith and Mafeking, 1900

"4th February – From General Sir. Redfers Buller to Field-Marshall Lord Roberts … I have today received your letter of 26 January. White keeps a stiff upper lip, but some of those under him are desponding. He calculates he has now 7000 effectives. They are eating their horses and have very little else. He expects to be attacked in force this week … "

The Backdrop

The Boer War is often regarded as one of the first truly modern wars, as the British Army, using traditional tactics, came close to being defeated by a Boer force which deployed what was almost a guerrilla strategy in punishing terrain.

The Book

Within weeks of the outbreak of fighting in South Africa, two sections of the British Army were besieged at Ladysmith and Mafeking. Split into two parts, the book begins with despatches describing the losses at Spion Kop on the way to rescue the garrison at Ladysmith, followed by the army report as the siege was lifted. In the second part is Lord Baden Powell's account of the siege of Mafeking and how the soldiers and civilians coped with the hardship and waited for relief to arrive.

ISBN 0 11 702408 2

The British Invasion Tibet: Colonel Younghusband, 1904

"On the 13th January I paid ceremonial visit to the Tibetans at Guru, six miles further down the valley in order that by informal discussion might assure myself of their real attitude. There were present at the interview three monks and one general from Lhasa … these monks were low-bred persons, insolent, rude and intensely hostile; the generals, on the other hand, were polite and well-bred."

The Backdrop

At the turn of the century, the British Empire was at its height, with its army in the forefront of the mission to bring what it saw as the tremendous civilising benefits of the British way of life to what it regarded as nations still languishing in the dark ages.

The Book

In 1901, a British Missionary Force under the leadership of Colonel Francis Younghusband crossed over the border from British India and invaded Tibet. Younghusband insisted on the presence of the Dalai Lama at meetings to give tribute to the British and their empire. The Dalai Lama merely replied that he must withdraw. Unable to tolerate such an insolent attitude, Younghusband marched forward and inflicted considerable defeats on the Tibetans in several onesided battles.

ISBN 0 11 702409 0

War 1914: Punishing the Serbs

" ... I said that this would make it easier for others such as Russia to counsel moderation in Belgrade. In fact, the more Austria could keep her demand within reasonable limits, and the stronger the justification she could produce for making any demands, the more chance there would be for smoothing things over. I hated the idea of a war between any of the Great Powers, and that any of them should be dragged into a war by Serbia would be detestable."

The Backdrop

In Europe before WW1, diplomacy between the Embassies was practised with a considered restraint and politeness which provided an ironic contrast to the momentous events transforming Europe forever.

The Book

Dealing with the fortnight leading up to the outbreak of the First World War, and mirroring recent events in Serbia to an astonishing extent. Some argued for immediate and decisive military action to punish Serbia for the murder of the Archduke Franz Ferdinand. Others pleaded that a war should not be fought over Serbia. The powers involved are by turn angry, conciliatory and, finally, warlike. Events take their course and history is changed.

ISBN 0 11 702410 4

War 1939: Dealing with Adolf Hitler

The Backdrop

As he presided over the rebuilding of a Germany shattered and humiliated after WW1, opinion as to Hitler and his intentions was divided and the question of whether his ultimate aim was military aggression by no means certain.

The Book

Sir Arthur Henderson, the British ambassador in Berlin in 1939 describes here, in his report to Parliament, the failure of his mission and the outbreak of war. He tells of his attempts to deal with both Hitler and von Ribbentrop to maintain peace and gives an account of the changes in German foreign policy regarding Poland.

ISBN 0 11 702411 2